NEGOTIATING SKILLS FOR BUSINESS

Better Management Skills

This highly popular range of inexpensive paperbacks covers all areas of basic management. Practical, easy to read and instantly accessible, these guides will help managers to improve their business or communication skills. Those marked * are available on audio cassette.

The books in this series can be tailored to specific company requirements. For further details, please contact the publisher, Kogan Page, telephone 0171 278 0433, fax 0171 837 6348.

NEGOTIATING SKILLS FOR BUSINESS

Elizabeth M Christopher

KOGAN
PAGE

27429

First published in 1996

Kogan Page Limited, 120 Pentonville Road, London N1 9JN

British Library Cataloguing in Publication Data
A CIP record for this book is available from the British Library.

ISBN 0 7494 1736 6

Typeset by BookEns Ltd., Royston, Herts.
Printed and bound in Great Britain by Clays Ltd, St Ives plc

Contents

Introduction

All organisational activity provides a setting for the fragile, sensitive and complicated business of negotiation. People negotiate with each other because they each want or need something from others but are unwilling or unable to take it by force or to fight for it. Negotiation is more involved with human relationships than is bargaining because more collaboration and coordination is required between the negotiating parties; and it is more than debate, which is only a part of negotiation. It is on a very high level of interpersonal communication and requires finely tuned skills.

The aims of this book are to help you identify these skills, to illustrate how they work in practice, and to demonstrate how, as a manager, you can acquire them. Because the personality of the negotiator is a critical element in all negotiation, this book discusses ways in which you can assess and develop your unique strengths as a negotiator. You will find exercises, questionnaires, examples and case studies to help you.

The focus of the book is on negotiation in organisational settings, but the concepts can be applied to more personal areas of human relationships. The objective of this book is to assist you to acquire power without aggression, persuasion without coercion, and achievement of your goals while at the same time promoting the satisfaction of other people.

Any method of negotiation may be fairly judged by three criteria:

- It should produce a wise agreement if agreement is possible.
- It should be efficient.
- It should improve or at least not damage the relationship between the parties.

A wise agreement can be defined as one which meets the legitimate interests of each side to the extent possible, resolves conflicting interests fairly, is durable, and takes community interests into account.

This book is written on the assumption that the following are basic characteristics of negotiation as a form of human behaviour:

1. Negotiation is a form of interpersonal communication. The human element is an essential component in all negotiation.
2. Negotiation requires the consenting involvement of at least two parties.
3. Negotiation is only possible if there is:

   - The need for a joint settlement of differences between the parties;
   - Acceptance by all parties that negotiation is the most satisfactory way to resolve their differences;
   - The belief, shared by all parties, that there is some possibility of a mutually acceptable compromise.

4. Negotiation implies that each party has some degree of power over the other.

These characteristics are discussed in detail in the following chapters, linked to specific examples and illustrated by exercises and case studies.

Finally, the writer hopes you will derive as much pleasure and benefit from this book as she did in researching and writing it.

CHAPTER 1
Your Individual Negotiation Style

After reading this chapter, you should be able to:

- Recognise the importance of identifying your own and others' personal priorities in negotiation;
- Identify your Individual Negotiation Style – your INS;
- Apply the characteristics of your INS to develop and broaden your inherent negotiation skills;
- Gain practice in analysing case studies of negotiation.

What are your priorities in negotiation?

Fisher and Ury, in their international bestseller *Getting to Yes*, advise you not to bargain over positions. Other writers on negotiation agree that the first priority is to avoid taking a fixed position in an argument because you will have difficulty if you need to move from it.

Case study

Jane Smith is an employee who has just asked her manager for a rise in salary. She has taken the position that the rise is well deserved because her sales figures are way over those originally set for her. Her manager in turn adopts the position that provision for such a rise was never in her contract. Jane insists that the contract stipulated a certain sales figure, which she has exceeded, therefore the terms of the contract are now irrelevant. The manager replies that the budget won't stand for remuneration changes to her contract.

In this kind of situation both parties will probably end up dissatisfied. Either the manager will feel resentful at having to pay Jane a higher salary, or Jane will feel undervalued and demotivated by having the request refused; and in either case each will feel exploited by the other. 'Interest', rather than 'positional', bargaining is likely to be more effective. If Jane and the manager had engaged in interest bargaining, the story might have been as follows:

Jane Smith asks the manager for a rise on the basis of her high sales figures. The manager agrees that it is in the company's interests that sales should be good and he expresses appreciation of her efforts. He asks her about her career plans and she tells him she would like to stay with the company and work towards a more senior management position. He encourages this ambition.

Then he reminds her that sales are seasonal, and one month's figures are not necessarily indicative of sales throughout the year. He points out that budgeting would be impossible if the salaries of all sales staff – who work to the same contract as Jane – were to be adjusted from month to month according to their sales figures.

Nevertheless, he is keen to reward good work, and suggests that if her performance is maintained over the year, he will discuss a new contract with a higher salary. Moreover, by that time she will be eligible to seek promotion. Thus, it is in everybody's interests for her to continue as she is doing now.

This is a good example of 'interest', as opposed to 'positional', bargaining. However, negotiation on this basis depends on two factors:

- You need to know exactly what you want, or at least what range of outcomes you are prepared to accept.
- You need to find out the other person's reasons for bargaining over the matter. People act for what seem like good reasons to them, but not to you; therefore, you have to convince the other party that the advantages *to them* of your proposal outweigh any apparent disadvantages.

This sounds good in theory, but unfortunately negotiation in real life doesn't always correspond to textbook examples. In practice, many of us are unclear about our own motives, let alone those of other people. How do you know what you *really* want as an outcome from a particular negotiation? And how can you judge what the other party is likely to find reasonable?

You may find interest bargaining more successful if you can identify your and the other party's *preferred negotiating style*. If so, you will become more aware of the kind of negotiation outcomes that are of first priority to them and to you. This will help you to work towards a compromise that will satisfy all parties. You will also learn to recognise where the other party is 'coming from' and the kind of compromises they are likely to think are in their best interests.

What kind of negotiator are you?

Like everybody, you are a unique individual. Nevertheless, personality tests suggest that people's preferred problem-solving behaviour seems to fall into broad patterns that can be grouped and categorised. Try the following quiz on yourself, your friends and colleagues, to give you some idea of the different ways people approach problem-solving and decision-making. You may be able to identify in yourself and others an Individual Negotiation Style (INS).

The INS quiz
Out of each set of four words, select *one* word with which you feel most comfortable. Don't agonise over each choice; make

your selection as quickly as you can, based on your immediate or intuitive response to the words.

1	6
a Results	a Efficiency
b Needs	b Controlling
c Procedures	c Grand designs
d Opportunities	d Feelings
2	**7**
a Concepts	a Moving ahead
b Performance	b Testing
c Planning	c Issues
d Motivation	d Team spirit
3	**8**
a Innovation	a Understanding
b Productivity	b Interdependence
c Organising	c Criteria
d Teamwork	d Priorities
4	**9**
a Creativity	a Empathy
b Facts	b The big picture
c People	c Task accomplishment
d Objectives	d Process
5	**10**
a Organising	a Rules
b Responsibility	b Consultation
c Possibilities	c Lateral thinking
d Communication	d Setting goals

Scoring
1a-1; 1b-3; 1c-2; 1d-4; 2a-4; 2b-1; 2c-2; 2d-3; 3a-4; 3b-1; 3c-2; 3d-3; 4a-4; 4b-2; 4c-3; 4d-1; 5a-2; 5b-1; 5c-4; 5d-3; 6a-1; 6b-2; 6c-4; 6d-3; 7a-1; 7b-2; 7c-4; 7d-3; 8a-3; 8b-4; 8c-1; 8d-2; 9a-3; 9b-4; 9c-1; 9d-2; 10a-2; 10b-3; 10c-4; 10d-1.

Assessment
Score 36–40. A high score suggests your INS may be that of an *Innovator*. If so, you may find that when engaged in negotiation you tend to:

- Think big; brainstorm ideas from the group, broaden people's perceptions of the problem;
- Generate a lot of options;
- Separate the people from the problem; refrain from attacking others' positions but rather look around and behind them;
- Refrain from taking things personally; or blaming other people for the problem;
- Ask open-ended questions; listen reflectively and withhold judgement;
- Encourage the other side to make suggestions;
- Focus on mutual interests, not individual positions, and avoid fixed bottom lines;
- Look for mutual gains.

People who seem naturally to adopt an Innovator style tend to ask questions beginning with 'Why ...?', such as: 'Why are we doing this?' and 'Why not do this ...?' They are inclined to explore many aspects of a situation, think in broad concepts, find new alternatives and opportunities and look for large, innovative and creative ways to solve problems.

However, they can be seen by others sometimes to be 'spacey' people, with their head in the clouds and unable to make decisions or take responsibility. Therefore, Innovators need to support their INS with good communication and fact-finding skills, and decisiveness in decision-making.

Score 26–35. A score that falls in this range suggests the negotiation style of a *Communicator*. When people adopt this INS in negotiation they tend to behave in the following ways:

- They don't plunge straight into negotiation but take time to build an atmosphere of trust, hospitality and sociability. They seek to build a working relationship;
- They are quick to select teams and hold briefing meetings; to establish roles;
- They like to display a united front and maintain a wide power base;

- They demonstrate understanding that emotions are legitimate; they allow people to let off steam, and explore their needs and concerns; show feelings, make people laugh, show impatience, frustration, pleasure;
- They recognise that negotiation is a relationship between the parties in which each must see the other's point of view;
- They give the other side a stake in the outcome: save face;
- They use symbolic statements, like thank-you notes and follow-up phone calls.

People who rely on a Communicator INS tend to ask 'Who?' rather than 'Why?' It is a people-oriented style that relies on communication, the building of relationships, teamwork and understanding people's needs. Such people tend to have strong values and beliefs, they consider feelings to be as important as facts, and they are good motivators. However, they can be seen by others sometimes as too emotional and judgmental. They need to support their style with listening skills (a strong Communicator INS is that of a talker rather than a listener), with facts as well as opinions, and decisions based on objective, rather than emotional, criteria.

Score 16–25. This range suggests the INS of *Processors*, who:

- Plan the negotiation; find out as much as possible about the other side; do their homework;
- Try to anticipate the other side's objections and strategies; explore possible concessions (may even role-play the negotiation in advance);
- Establish an agenda and negotiate by objectives;
- Resist time pressures;
- Negotiate on issues, not personalities;
- Focus on facts, legitimacy; quote precedents, use statistics, refer to experts;
- Define limits, stick to the agenda, limit their own authority to make final decisions;
- Avoid getting personal;
- Ask for, and put, things in writing.

People with a Processor INS tend to ask 'How should we do this?' rather than 'Why are we doing it?' or 'Who will be involved?' It is a style that relies on facts and proofs rather than feelings, on order and method, planning and procedures, and the testing of ideas before they are put into practice. However, Processors can be seen by others sometimes as fussy and pedantic, rule-bound, tied up with 'red tape' and too slow to make decisions. Therefore, they need to consider feelings as well as facts, to look at broad perspectives as well as detail, and to consider change and innovation as well as established guidelines.

Score 10–15. A low score suggests the INS of *Activators*, who:

- Are most often referred to as 'business-like';
- Speak clearly and to the point;
- Ask questions to obtain more information and explanation;
- Listen actively for shades of meaning;
- Think 'on their feet', which means they are quick to devise alternatives, even on the spur of the moment;
- Distrust ambiguity, prefer forms of agreement (minutes, contracts, etc);
- Take the total environment into account, which means that their decisions tend to be situation-specific. An Activator style is essentially pragmatic: their bottom line is 'Will this work?';
- Don't make excuses for problems; use objective standards of problem-solving;
- Are prepared to concede smaller demands in exchange for agreement over bigger ones.

People who own an Activator INS are inclined to ask 'What are we going to do?' rather than 'Why are we doing it?', 'How should we do it?' or 'Who is involved?' It is an action style that welcomes (and often creates) challenges and change, identifies objectives, makes decisions and looks for results. People with this style like to take responsibility for setting and achieving goals; they value efficiency and productivity. They rely heavily on feedback from others and their own experience of similar situations in the past. However, Activators can be seen sometimes as 'pushy', even aggressive. Therefore, they need to consider others' feelings, to cultivate patience and to delay decisions until they have accumulated a wide variety of relevant information.

Case studies

Read the following case studies and answer the questions after each pair. Then turn to Chapter 6 for some suggestions.

1. The Salk vaccine

Dr Jonas Salk, who died in June 1995, became an international hero when he developed the first polio vaccine. He was working at the University of Pittsburgh in the 1950s and overcame the resistance of scientific doubters who said it couldn't be done. He incorporated the results of his own and others' more traditional research and went on to create an effective vaccine by the use of killed virus. In 1955, after the vaccine was officially given the go-ahead, the polio toll plummeted.

2. Western Power

Electricity supplier Western Power needed urgently to cut off the electricity for a short period on the 66,000 volt feed line that runs through the Australian NSW country town of Coonamble. The plan was to cut the supply on 24 June 1995. However, one of the technicians pointed out that if the plan were to go ahead on the proposed date and time, it would prevent everybody in the small town from watching the Rugby World Cup Final – a deprivation that would be keenly felt by virtually the whole community. His senior manager became very defensive because he felt under attack for making what would obviously be a very unpopular decision; but the technician argued that everybody would benefit if Western Power were to install a generator in the well-patronised Coonamble pub so all who wanted to, could follow the game.

Questions

Bearing in mind that all IN styles overlap to some extent, both these case studies are argued to illustrate a style of negotiation that is primarily that of Innovators. List three kinds of behaviour in each case that appear to demonstrate an Innovator INS:

Case study 1

(a)_____

(b)_____

(c)_____

Case study 2

(a)_____

(b)_____

(c)_____

3. The union rep and the works manager

Stephen is the recently elected union representative and John is the works supervisor. Stephen favours an informal, relationship-based method of discussing industrial problems, while John likes to follow agreed procedures.

The first time Stephen had a union problem, he walked into John's office with a request for 'a chat' and then wasted a lot of time, as John saw it, before coming to the point of his visit. John then refused to discuss the matter until Stephen had put it in writing. Stephen lost his temper and stormed out of John's office, threatening industrial action over what they both knew was a minor matter that could have been easily and informally settled.

John consulted his manager, who suggested that maybe if his manner to Stephen were more friendly, they might start the discussion again on a better footing. So John asked Stephen to see him again, then greeted him warmly, invited him to sit down and offered him a cup of tea. Stephen was taken aback at first, but he sat down and John came from behind his desk to sit beside him. The discussion was amicable and productive, and when Stephen got up to leave, he said: 'You know, you're really not a bad guy after all!'

4. Lethal weapons

In the police force in Britain in 1995 most chief constables favoured the general arming of police officers. However, 79 per cent of police officers who were polled by the Police Federation rejected the idea; and government focus has now shifted towards an increase in specialist armed units instead of routinely arming patrolling officers.

Questions
Bearing in mind that all IN styles overlap to some extent, both these case studies are argued to illustrate a style of negotiation that is primarily that of Communicators. List at least three kinds of behaviour in each case that appear to demonstrate a Communicator INS:

Case study 3

(a) _____

(b) _____

(c) _____

Case study 4

(a) _____

(b) _____

(c) _____

5. The parking permit

Sally joined a communal household because she wanted to save rent. The house was on a busy main road and parking was allowed only for car owners who held a residents' permit.

When Sally went to the local council office to get a permit she was asked to provide proof of residency in the form of a gas, electricity or telephone bill. She explained that the lease of the house was in the name of another person who lived there, and all the bills were in this person's name, but she showed the official a number of letters addressed to her at the house. She explained she was on her lunch break and that her time was very limited.

However, the official insisted that rules were rules, and in this case the relevant rule specified the production of a bill. The official was so uncompromising that Sally accused her of taking personal pleasure in her denial — an accusation which the woman indignantly denied.

Sally finally burst into tears, which attracted the attention of another officer who tried to persuade his colleague that Sally had shown sufficient proof of residency, but the woman was adamant that she had no authority to make that kind of decision, and that Sally should refer the matter to the department manager, in writing. That afternoon Sally did so, and eventually obtained her permit.

6. Marathon run

Fourteen-year-old Peter Molloy wanted to run in an annual marathon held in his town; and he wanted all his family to run with him. This included his father and mother and his three brothers, aged 16, 12 and 10, his adopted sister aged 15, and a cousin who lived with them, aged 14.

Nobody wanted to join him. They made all sorts of excuses — they weren't fit enough or fast enough, the distance was too long, they would be making fools of themselves, and so on. However, Peter presented the following information to his family: the distance was 10 miles but the rules allowed a generous time to complete the course; people of all ages, shapes, sizes and degrees of fitness regularly took part; it was a family fun run rather than a competitive event; and the local gym conducted training sessions at a very reasonable rate for people who wanted to get fit enough in time to compete.

His information was so comprehensive he was able to overcome all objections and finally everybody in the family ran with him, and his 16-year-old brother completed the event in a respectable 73 minutes.

Questions
Bearing in mind that all IN styles overlap to some extent, both these case studies are argued to illustrate a style of negotiation that is primarily that of Processors. List at least three kinds of behaviour in each case that appear to demonstrate a Processor INS:

Case study 5

(a) _____

(b)_____

(c) _____

Case study 6

(a) _____

(b)_____

(c) _____

7. The rented van

Hassan ran a van rental service. One day a woman wanted to rent a van to move some furniture. Hassan informed her that although the driver's section of the van and the engine were insured, the cab itself was not. He emphasised this, explaining clearly that the cab was so high that drivers had to be very careful to check for low overhead obstacles, and that she would be fully responsible for any damage to the cab.

The woman told him she was accustomed to driving all kinds of vehicles and prided herself on her skill. Hassan listened carefully and concluded that she might be over-confident. He asked her about the locations where she would be driving and whether there would be low obstacles and she told him, no. He asked her if her driving licence had ever been endorsed, and again she said no. Finally, he insisted she read through the contract before signing it and watched her drive away. He then telephoned a panel-beater friend and made a tentative booking for the van over the next couple of days.

The following day the woman returned the van with the cab badly damaged. She had driven down a driveway to her new apartment without stopping to think that the tall van might not fit under the overhanging balcony of the flat on the first floor. The repair estimate came to £300 but Hassan gave the woman a discount in exchange for cash.

8. The TV episode

In 1993 TV director Karl Hermann won an award for a documentary examining the effects of AIDS on the arts community in his city.

A year later he was involved in a dispute over his direction of an episode of a popular, long-running TV soap opera. The writers wanted to include a scene where an AIDS patient asks a sympathetic gay doctor to carry out an act of euthanasia for him, even though he still has several months to live.

The producers objected to the scene on the grounds that it might alienate regular viewers of the family-oriented series. Karl suggested that the episode would be less controversial if the doctor were female and heterosexual, and offered to make the casting change. The producers were still doubtful, so he reminded them that under his direction the 1993 AIDS documentary had received a General Viewing certificate. The producers were aware that this programme had won an award and were willing to trust to his experience. The episode went ahead in its altered form and won an award in its turn.

Questions
Bearing in mind that all IN styles overlap, these case studies illustrate a style of negotiation that is primarily Activator. List three kinds of behaviour in each case that appear to demonstrate an Activator INS:

Case study 7

(a) _____

(b) _____

(c) _____

Case study 8

(a) _____

(b) _____

(c) _____

Now turn to Chapter 6 for a discussion of these case studies.

CHAPTER 2
Talking and Listening

After reading this chapter, you should be able to:

- Explain why poor listening skills constitute a common cause of breakdown in negotiation;
- List effective listening behaviours;
- Isolate the components of critical listening;
- Identify distractions to effective listening, and how to avoid them;
- Discuss the need for feedback in negotiation;
- Make effective notes during negotiations;
- Apply a 'stress formula' for stress management;
- Become more proficient in paraphrasing and rewording statements to obtain agreement between negotiating parties.

Talking too much and listening too little

Probably the most common cause of breakdown in negotiation is when parties talk too much and listen too little. Learning to listen to what the other is 'really' saying is essential when searching for common ground and acceptable compromises. Common guidelines in the literature on listening skills can be summarised as a checklist of 'dos' and 'don'ts':

(a) Establish good understanding by asking questions,

paraphrasing statements, repeating points to be sure of agreement. In general, speak clearly in short, clear statements with pauses in between so people can interject questions or comments without appearing rude.

(b) Ask for confirmation of understanding or agreement.

(c) Build rapport with the other person or people. Adapt your manner and tone of voice to suit the setting. Learn something about them before you meet them.

(d) Identify any obvious barriers to listening. For example, do you tend to dominate a conversation? Ask your friends to tell you frankly if you talk too much and listen too little!

(e) Create a comfortable environment for listening. Avoid distractions such as interruptions and noise, people coming and going, phones ringing all the time.

Asking questions

Sometimes you will find yourself answering one question with another — not to score points but to increase the amount and quality of the feedback. The following dialogue is an example:

Dialogue: Flexible hours

UNION REP	We want to return to the matter of flexibility in working hours. Why aren't you prepared to discuss it?
MANAGEMENT REP	Can you explain to us why you give such a high priority to this item on the agenda?
UNION REP	We know that you give a higher priority to the problem of undue absenteeism. We acknowledge the seriousness of this; but we suggest that if you were to introduce a trial scheme under which relevant employees are free, within defined limits, to choose their working hours, then the absentee problem would solve itself. Why don't you give it a try?

MANAGEMENT REP   But what about the overtime pay that such a scheme would entail? We can't afford it.

UNION REP   If we can reach agreement on the question of overtime, would you be prepared to trial the scheme?

MANAGEMENT REP   What sort of agreement have you in mind?

And so on. This example illustrates how debate can be enlarged and then focused by asking questions, listening and responding to answers.

The need for feedback

A question-and-answer example is one way to illustrate that communication is a two-way process. Senders must have feedback from receivers to ensure messages have been understood as intended. There are other ways to demonstrate this. For instance, there is an entertaining game called *Listening*.* It takes about half an hour to play, with a group of people of almost any size. Play it with colleagues, friends or family to demonstrate that merely listening to instructions is not enough for people to understand what they have to do: they need feedback on their progress.

Listening
These are your instructions as group leader:

1. Give a blank sheet of paper to each participant.
2. Ask everybody to close their eyes and keep them closed until further notice.
3. Ask them, still with their eyes closed, to fold the sheet of paper. Don't answer questions, just repeat the instruction.
4. Tell them to tear off the top right-hand corner.

---

* Devised by Sleigh, John, *Making Learning Fun*, and adapted by Christopher, EM and Smith, LE, *Negotiation Training Through Gaming: Strategies, Tactics and Manœuvres.*

5. Say: 'Fold the sheet of paper'.
6. 'Tear the bottom left-hand corner'.
7. 'Fold the sheet of paper'.
8. 'Tear off the top left-hand corner'.
9. If the group is large, say: 'Before you open your eyes, raise your hand if you have followed all the instructions'.
10. Then ask everybody to open their eyes and compare their sheet of paper with those of others.

Almost inevitably there will be major differences between people's end-products from the exercise. Ask everybody what was missing from the communication process; and the answer, of course, is feedback. After playing this game, the group can discuss ways to improve the quality of their communication and enhance their own capacity to interpret others' messages.

Critical listening

You will have been encouraged at school and college to evaluate critically everything you *read*: to consider the context, content and organisation of the information; the author's purpose and intended readership; the main themes, key points and arguments; the kind of evidence the author presents; and so on. However, it is easy to overlook the need also to evaluate critically what you *hear*. The following example is one instance where good listening skills may be critical to the success of a negotiation.

The planning committee
You have been asked at very short notice to sit on a planning committee in place of your colleague who is away sick. You have had no time to study the proposals under discussion but several of them are relevant to your department and at least one – concerning parking rights for staff members – will affect your department adversely if it is adopted. You ask that the relevant proposals be deferred to the next meeting so that your colleague can speak to them but the chair-holder and committee members insist that discussion and voting take

place now. You will need to listen hard to evaluate the implications of what you are about to hear. What strategies should you employ for critical listening?

Think about this for five minutes and list some suggestions before turning to Chapter 6 for comments.

In the above situation I would adopt the following tactics:

1. _____

2. _____

3. _____

4. _____

In Chapter 4 you will find a detailed discussion of the organisational and individual sources from which negotiators draw power. One of those sources is *knowledge*. The above 'hypothetical' illustrates how much stronger your critical listening skills would be if you had at least some knowledge of how this committee works and what kind of leeway you are entitled to demand. People who know the rules and procedures that govern a particular situation often control it. Next time, study the *context* in which you will have to operate. You will be surprised how much more effectively you can employ critical listening to support or refute others' arguments if you know the rules of the game!

Notetaking

Notebook headings
A. Headings that relate to the *context* of the information:

PURPOSE?: What is my informant's *purpose* in telling me this? For example, might it be to persuade me about something? To inform me? To impress me? What?

FOR WHOM was this information originally gathered? What vested interests might be at work here?

ORGANISATION? How is the information *organised*? How logical is the argument?

B. Headings that relate to the *content* of the information:

MAIN ARGUMENT: What is my informant's *main theme* or *argument*? What is this person *really* trying to tell me?

KEY POINTS: What are the *key points* that support my informant's arguments?

EVIDENCE: What *evidence* is provided for statements made by my informant? Is the evidence *fact* or *opinion*? How credible is it?

ASSUMPTIONS: What *assumptions* is my informant making? Are they open to question?

IRRELEVANCIES: Is there any *irrelevant information*? For example, is my informant trying to distract me with emotional but irrelevant appeals to my feelings?

If you learn to evaluate what you hear in this systematic way, you will become much more critical as a listener and therefore a more effective negotiator. Notetaking is a very useful aid in this respect, provided you use notes sparingly and methodically.

General aims in notetaking during negotiation
- To have a record of main ideas/arguments/discussion.
- To record examples, precedents, statistics.
- To record definitions, special terms or vocabularies.
- To provide ammunition for later questions and discussion about the content and context of the information provided by the other party.
- To use in preparing a report of the negotiation.

Distractions to effective listening

The following is a checklist of distractions that will hinder your skills as a negotiator because they counteract your ability to listen retentively:

- Not enough time;
- Becoming stressed;
- Unsure of goals;

- Noise;
- Can't say no;
- Interruptions, phone calls;
- Pressures of work;
- Taking a fixed position;
- Personal problems: bias and prejudice; guilt or shame; fear of change; anger;
- Breakdown in understanding.

Not enough time?
Any kind of time pressure will adversely affect your ability to listen to and evaluate what you hear. Part of your self-training in negotiation should include time management!

Becoming stressed?
Some people's listening skills actually improve under pressure. Such people like deadlines and the excitement of meeting them; the rush of adrenalin sharpens their senses. Others find stress a real barrier to listening. If you are one of the latter, consider the following:

1. The more *control* you have over the situation, the easier it is for you to ask the speaker to slow down, to repeat or paraphrase information until you feel you understand it; and the easier it will be to argue your case persuasively. Increase your sense of control!
2. The more *important* you feel your listening to be, the more you are likely to feel stressed in trying to retain it. If you can reduce the importance to you of a particular situation — for example by studying the subject in advance, or with the support of a colleague — your frame of mind will be more relaxed. Keep things in perspective!
3. The more *difficult* the task, the more stress you will feel. If you can increase your knowledge of the task and what will be entailed to accomplish it, you will feel less stressed. Reduce task difficulty. Make things as easy for yourself as you can!
4. The fewer *constraints* you have on the *time available*, the less

stressed you will be. Ask for more time if you need it. Say, for example, that you have to consult a senior colleague before you can comment on the information you have heard. Learn to manage your time!

Unsure of goals?

How sure are you that negotiation is *your preferred method* of achieving what you want? Maybe you don't have the temperament to bargain? Maybe you don't really like bargaining and therefore your commitment to a particular outcome is not very strong in terms of the time and effort you are willing to devote to it. If, feeling this way, you nevertheless have to negotiate on behalf of others, you may have to increase your level of commitment. You may be able to do so by concentrating, not on your own interests but on those of the people you represent. This includes consulting them and making sure of their support before and during the negotiation.

On the other hand, you may now recognise that bargaining is something you enjoy as a game and to which you can bring particular strengths because the *process* of the activity – including the social interaction – is as important, or more important, to you than the *end result*.

In any case, you should now feel clearer about your motivation for negotiation and your strengths as a negotiator. Such recognition should improve your listening skills to a remarkable extent because now you know what you are listening for!

Noise?

Some people find background noise is stimulating. Others flourish in the relatively impersonal, calm atmosphere of the conference table. If noise distracts you from listening effectively to what is being said, try to eliminate it as much as possible. Ask for the window to be closed if the traffic is heavy outside. Choose a time of day when noise from surrounding rooms will be at its lowest. If the noise is temporary, discuss the least controversial items on the agenda while it lasts.

Can't say no?
You cannot listen and evaluate suggestions and proposals if you fear to offend people or hurt their feelings by having to say no to distracting chatter. Keep your objectives clear in your mind and find tactful ways of saying no!

Interruptions, phone calls?
You can't listen attentively if you are constantly distracted by these interferences to your concentration. Make it clear to your secretary or whoever is responsible that you cannot take calls while you are in conference.

Pressures of work?
You have to find ways to combine existing responsibilities with the negotiation work you have undertaken. Otherwise you will listen to the negotiation with half an ear because you are distracted by thoughts of what's going wrong in your office in your absence. Establish your goals for the negotiation and organise your time, as suggested above!

Taking a fixed position?
You will be a poor listener to the extent that you have closed your mind to all compromise not in accord with your fixed position in the debate. Chapter 1 discussed the advantages of 'interest bargaining' compared with 'positional bargaining'. Your listening skills will improve if you concentrate on the search for mutual interests.

Personal problems?
These seriously affect everybody's listening skills. Don't try to handle them on your own. Talk to family, friends, colleagues. There are also personal barriers such as:

- Denial (not wanting to admit you have a problem);
- Bias and prejudice (eg for or against individuals or groups of people);
- Pain and illness;
- Guilt and shame;

- Fear of change;
- Anger.

It is impossible to keep emotion out of the most impersonal negotiation. However, you can use self-knowledge to control unruly feelings.

Lastly, on the subject of personal barriers to listening: keep in good health, take exercise, watch your diet; and strive for peace of mind!

Breakdown in understanding?

If you don't understand what is required of you, you can't focus on listening. Failure to understand something in the context of a negotiation may not be your responsibility. Communication is a two-way process and unfortunately some people have never learned to express themselves clearly. Moreover, texts and instructions are not always clearly described. For example, you may come across agenda items that have too broad a meaning ('Discussion of enterprise bargaining'); also vague generalisations ('Human resource management in cross-cultural contexts'). If you are not clear about the real meaning of an item to be negotiated, discuss it with the parties to the debate until you are sure you understand what is required of you. Another method for gaining more understanding of the negotiation issues is to paraphrase and reword what you hear.

Paraphrasing and rewording for greater persuasion power

People often give mixed messages, even when they intend to be crystal clear. Sometimes these confusions have their origin in cross-cultural misunderstandings. For example, British managers are likely to mean 'Yes' or 'No' when they say so. Japanese managers are more likely to mean 'Go on, I'm listening!' when they say 'Yes' and 'You are not stating the position as we would like it to be!' when they say 'No'. Hence the importance of rewording and paraphrasing what people tell you, to make sure you are all on the same wavelength.

Finally, here are some examples for rewording statements you might want to make but which might sound too blunt.

STATEMENT   We will probably have to make decisions that affect you, without consulting you.

REWORDING   It is not practical to make a rigid rule that we consult you before making any decision that might affect you. There may be times when we have to act on our own initiative.

STATEMENT   I think you're talking nonsense!

REWORDING   I don't think I've understood the sense of what you've just said. Let me repeat what I think you mean, and you can correct me if I've got it wrong.

(Note that this example demonstrates the advantage in negotiation of accepting responsibility for lack of understanding rather than blaming the other party – even when it is obvious the other party is in fact talking nonsense!)

STATEMENT   You're asking for everything and offering nothing in return!

PARAPHRASE You're asking for a very large concession. We might consider it if you were to offer ... in exchange.

STATEMENT   How do I know I can trust you?

PARAPHRASE What kind of guarantees can you offer?

STATEMENT   You might at least have the decency to arrive on time for our meeting. I've been waiting here for half an hour!

REWORDING   I notice that for this meeting there was half an hour's difference between our respective times of arrival. Would you prefer a later time for our next meeting?

(Note that this tactic puts the responsibility on to the other parties for setting the time of meeting, therefore it is more likely that they will stick to the time they themselves stipulated.)

CHAPTER 3
Handling Conflict in Negotiation

Negotiation requires the consenting involvement of at least two parties; the need for joint settlement of differences; acceptance by all parties that negotiation is the most satisfactory way to resolve their differences; a belief, shared by all parties, that there is some possibility of a mutually acceptable compromise; and some degree of power that each party has over the other.

After reading this chapter you should be able to:

- Describe some tactics for harmonising conflict, based on an understanding of two fundamental views of the nature of conflict;
- Analyse case studies of unexpected conflict;
- Identify methods of handling these crises, based on your INS;
- List a number of factors likely to lead to stressful situations;
- Apply the stress formula on page 45 to avoid or minimise potential conflict;
- Describe a number of methods for preventing small conflicts from growing into big ones;
- Discuss the implications of others seeing you as a source of potential conflict; and how to avoid this;
- Become more sensitive to the presence of hidden agendas –

and therefore potential conflict – under apparently peaceful offers;

- Probe for details in negotiations where the results will materially affect you, in order to avoid conflict later.

The nature of conflict

Why does conflict occur when common sense urges peaceful cooperation as the most effective method for people to live and work together? There are two general and mutually opposing views of the nature of human conflict:

1. Harmony between people and groups is 'natural' and 'good'. Conflict is harmful and 'bad'. Its presence means there is something wrong with the relationship between the respective parties. Those who cause the conflict are misguided, wicked or emotionally disturbed. They must be corrected by gentle or harsh means in order to re-establish a 'normal' state of harmony and balance.
2. Conflict is inevitable and not necessarily harmful. On the contrary, some conflict can be stimulating – such as competition – and will contribute to the overall good of all parties involved. No matter what the conflict, it can be managed to minimise losses and maximise gains for everybody.

If you are to be a negotiator, then by definition you must hold the second view because negotiation requires joint settlement of differences through consenting involvement by all power-holders and their acceptance that compromise is possible. Therefore, your motto as a negotiator is: *whatever the conflict, nobody is wrong!* Your business is to resolve disagreements in your own best interests (or the best interests of those you serve) and in the hope that this will also be in the best interests of the other parties.

When disputes between people are not recognised as inevitable and essentially healthy manifestations of human endeavour, to be worked through constructively for the eventual good of all concerned, they will escalate into some kind of warfare. The ultimate disaster from such escalation is the loss of human lives. At the very least it will result in stress for the participants, misallocation of resources to mutually destructive activities such as strikes and sabotage, and diminished performance by everybody concerned. Any talk (or thoughts) of 'right' or 'wrong' are irrelevant in the face of risks such as these, which arise when one party projects its own values on to the other.

For example, sales staff think production staff 'should be' quicker to produce the goods they sell. The production people think the sales people 'should not' make contracts for delivery of goods without consideration of production times. Each group believes it is right and the other party is wrong. The results are stressed-out workers, dissatisfied customers and reduced profitability. Compromise does not lie in judging between the disputing parties but in accommodating both. Measures might include:

- Job rotation, whereby production workers spend some time in sales, and vice versa. This gives both a 'feel' for each others' problems;
- Rewording the company's standard contracts with customers to allow for production lead times. This might take some of the stress off the production team;
- Reviewing production methods: can they be improved?
- Reviewing the communication process between production and sales units: how can it be made more effective?
- Rewards, by way of bonuses, to the production team for shortening production times; and to the sales team for reduction in customer complaints.

These suggestions are all based on the premise that you cannot alter other people's behaviour by imposing on them the same values and driving forces by which you act. Instead, learn their values and what drives them (the need for success? For power? For recognition?), then find ways to give them what they want (or to offer a desirable alternative) that also satisfies you.

There is another motto that may help you handle conflict as

an inevitable part of the negotiation process: *there is never one single source of conflict; and nobody who is involved in it in any way can be neutral.* Two of the most effective techniques in negotiation are to *identify the various sources* of a particular conflict; and to *identify everybody who is a party to it.* Only then can you try to persuade all parties to compromise on some issues in order to obtain concessions on others. The problem is not to get the parties to communicate, but to get them to communicate effectively about *issues where there are opportunities for agreement.* All too often these issues are clouded by preconceptions that run counter to the argument that whatever the conflict, nobody is wrong! Such preconceptions include the following:

(a) *Mirror-image.* Each party regards the other's position as opposite to their own, and inimical to it. Therefore, both parties are blind to opportunities for accommodation or compromise.

(b) *Different interpretation of the same facts or actions.* The parties only see what they want to see and favour whatever interpretation they regard as most compatible with their predetermined ends.

(c) *Double standards.* The parties judge their own acts by a different standard from that which they apply to their adversaries.

(d) *Polarised single-issue positions.* The parties each focus on one issue that concerns them and one source of information, and see their task as forcing their adversaries to surrender unconditionally.

Promoting consensus in negotiation

In real-life negotiations, there are a number of actions you can take to encourage objective problem-solving between the parties, as follows:

1. Establish an atmosphere in which people feel free to raise objections.
2. When asking opinions, don't define the results you expect.

3. In large-scale and lengthy negotiations, set up parallel, independent policy-making groups or committees.
4. If necessary, periodically divide these groups into sub-groups.
5. Have representatives of each group act in liaison with the other groups.
6. Invite experts who are not members of the group to challenge the views of core members.
7. Encourage someone to play devil's advocate.
8. Try to think like your competition.
9. Before ratifying any decision, hold a second meeting to rethink the issue and explore any residual doubts.

In spite of the most careful planning, however, the unexpected will always occur. Therefore, the next topic for discussion is that of *crisis management*.

Crisis management: negotiating the unexpected

First, choose which ending you *prefer* to the following story. The only criterion for choice is that you pick the one you like best – that appeals to you most – although perhaps in real life you might adopt any one of the suggested courses of action, combine some elements from each or do something quite different, depending on the circumstances. Then turn to Chapter 6 for comments.

Narrative 1. Double booking

> John booked a conference room in a hotel for an important meeting with company branch heads from all over the city. He arrived 15 minutes before the meeting was due to start, only to find that the hotel had overlooked his reservation and no room was available.

Which of the following endings appeals to you most?

Possible ending (A)

The hotel manager, Kim, apologised but disclaimed responsibility. John replied that he understood the best-laid plans could go wrong, and asked what had happened in this instance. When Kim realised he was not going to make trouble, she explained willingly that a social club meeting had a regular monthly booking for the conference room, but the hotel employee who spoke to John didn't realise this, being new to the job. The mistake was not picked up until shortly before John arrived. She told him the Primrose Club was a small group that met regularly in the hotel and afterwards spent some time in the bar.

John asked to see the conference room and the bar. Then he suggested the conference room was rather large and formal for such a small and friendly group. Maybe they would like to hold their meeting in the bar? There was plenty of room in one of the big alcoves, especially since very few customers were in the bar at that time of day.

Kim liked the novelty of the idea. Several members of the Club arrived at that moment, and greeted with pleasure the change of location for their assembly. John had a drink with them to celebrate and enjoyed himself so much he was late for his own meeting in the conference room. Afterwards he thanked Kim, and made some helpful suggestions to avoid double bookings in future. Thereafter he became one of Kim's favourite customers.

Response
I like this ending because:

_____

_____

I feel dissatisfied with this ending because:

_____

_____

Possible ending (B)

Kim apologised but disclaimed responsibility. John expressed his feelings forcibly and they exchanged some heated words. He insisted she had a responsibility to help him out. What would his colleagues think of him, and of the hotel, if they arrived to find things in such a mess? These appeals moved Kim to telephone a nearby restaurant. The manager was a friend of hers and offered her the private use of an upstairs room. When the business visitors arrived it was a simple matter for everybody to walk the short distance to the restaurant. The following day John telephoned Kim to thank her and sent her some beautiful flowers. Kim asked him to talk to her personally should he wish to use the hotel facilities in future, and she would oversee all arrangements.

Response
I like this ending because:

_____

_____

I feel dissatisfied with this ending because:

_____

_____

Possible ending (C)

Kim apologised but disclaimed responsibility. John replied that he had a verbal contract with the hotel, which was probably enforceable by law, but which she had now broken at risk of the hotel eventually having to pay damages for loss of his business as a result of the hotel's mistake. Having clearly established his rights as a consumer, he specified his requirements: a quiet and private room to seat eight people for a meeting which was due to begin very soon and would last two hours at the most.

Kim was intimidated by John's air of authority and asked if he would consider holding his meeting in the sitting room of one of the hotel guest suites. She would put extra chairs in the room and arrange for refreshments to be served. John agreed to these concessions and the meeting proceeded as originally planned. However, he made a mental note that the hotel booking arrangements were unreliable and decided not to use it again. On her part, Kim was resentful that John had taken such a hard line and instructed her staff to make some excuse to refuse him, should he want to use the hotel facilities in future.

Response
I like this ending because:

_____

_____

I feel dissatisfied with this ending because:

_____

_____

Possible ending (D)

Kim apologised but disclaimed responsibility. However, as soon as John ascertained the facts he didn't waste time blaming anybody but moved swiftly into action, took a quick tour of the hotel, identified a quiet section of the dining room and announced he would hold his meeting there. He suggested that free refreshments would be a gracious gesture by Kim to make up for her negligence, and she agreed. In fact, John was not unduly worried because he was a resourceful person who could almost always work his way out of a crisis. On this occasion he reflected that if the worst came to the worst he could take his colleagues by taxi to his company office, trusting to luck that the boardroom would be free that afternoon. He made a mental note to charge the taxi to the hotel.

Kim appreciated John's business-like attitude to the whole affair – particularly as he had taken all the responsibility for solving the problem. She assured him that she would overhaul the hotel booking system so that double bookings could not occur again. John accepted this and told her he would use the hotel for one more function, when the need arose. If arrangements were satisfactory he would forget about this present crisis; but if there should be another upset to his arrangements he would never use the hotel again.

Response
I like this ending because:

_____

_____

I feel dissatisfied with this ending because:

_____

_____

Now turn to the discussion of this case study in Chapter 6.

How to prevent small conflicts growing into big ones

People whose jobs are potentially life-threatening to themselves and others – like airline pilots – argue that no major accident happens in isolation. There is always a chain of small mishaps, each one almost insignificant in itself, but uncorrected they will amount to disaster. Hence the rigid system of checks that every pilot follows before take-off.

It is part of your job as a negotiator to try to prevent small conflicts from escalating into major disputes. Imagine you read the following report in your local newspaper. Then answer the questions that follow it:

Teachers hit by stress toll

Children at the local primary school, which has 30 teachers and more than 500 pupils, played in the school grounds last week oblivious of the trouble brewing among their teachers since the beginning of the year. Principal Mary Robinson has been on sick leave for six months and ten staff members have taken stress leave in the past eight months. A Ministry of Education representative confirmed that several teachers are seeking compensation for stress-related illnesses and an independent investigation will be held to determine the causes. Apparently, the school has experienced a range of unusual circumstances over the past year, including long periods of maintenance work on buildings, the school being split into two sites, and the introduction of new teachers.

'The school is now spread across two sites, which has led to communication problems between teaching and administrative staff,' said the deputy principal. 'Also we have had some new staff members who have different values, ideas and teaching methods from the rest of us, and these have had to be worked through.'

Fred Everett, president of the school's Parents and Teachers' Association, said he was aware some teachers had taken stress leave but he hadn't been told what was being done 'behind the scenes' to resolve the issues.

'The school has a transient population and has up to 600 pupils at any given time,' he said. 'Sometimes we get up to 250 and 300 students coming and going because this is a holiday resort area. That can put a huge strain on the administration of the school and the teachers because students don't settle in and teachers don't know where they're up to with their school work.'

While picking up her daughter, Emma, from school last week, Mrs Jones said problems among teachers had been 'kept under wraps'.

'All this is having a bad impact on my daughter's studies,' she said. 'Emma complains that her teacher is always in a bad temper because the school is so short-staffed and she has so many students to deal with. If the teachers are stressed out then parents have a right to know. If people are under stress they can fly off the handle a lot easier.'

Questions

1. List the factors that have caused such stress in the school.

_____

_____

_____

2. What measures could have been taken to avoid the situation the school is now in?

_____

_____

_____

Now turn to Chapter 6 for some answers.

Dealing with conflict-related stress

Apply the following stress formula to this situation.

S   = the degree of Stress experienced in a given situation.

LC = Lack of Control by individuals over the situation.

IO   = The Importance to individuals of the Outcome of the situation.

DT = The Difficulty of the Task to be accomplished.

CTA = Constraints on the Time Available for task accomplishment.

Then: $S = LC \times IO \times DT \times CTA$.

If any of the above factors can be reduced, stress overall will be reduced. 'Teachers hit by stress toll' is an example of a large-scale conflict that could have been minimised by the application of this formula. For example:

LC: Lack of control

The teachers obviously felt their lack of control over the situation of a fluctuating student population, with transient students feeling unsettled, and the difficulty of assessing their various educational levels. More control could have been imposed by the employment of specialist staff to assess the needs of these short-term, transient students. Thus, teacher stress could have been avoided.

IO: Reducing the importance of outcomes

Teachers have a great deal of professional and ethical capital invested in their teaching methods and the outcomes they hope to obtain in terms of student learning. If these values are threatened, considerable conflict and stress are likely to result. An orientation programme for new teachers to integrate their values and methods with those current in the school might reduce differences between perceptions of outcomes and thus avoid stress.

DT: Reducing task difficulty

A major problem appears to have been that of communication between the administrative and teaching staff in the respective sites. This difficulty could have been avoided by changing the organisational structure of the school. One suggestion is that small, semi-autonomous teams might have been formed, each team to be located on the same site, each consisting of a mixture of teaching and administrative staff members.

CTA: Extending the time

There seem to have been two major time constraints. One concerned the length of time the normal life of the school was disrupted by building work; and the other was due to teachers being overworked because of staff shortages and therefore being unable to spend as much time as they felt necessary with each student. The latter constraint was a direct result of many of their colleagues being absent on sick leave because of stress caused by the situation in general. The problem with disruption due to lengthy maintenance work could have been avoided by setting priorities for maintenance work on buildings, so the work could be organised in time stages to cause as little disruption as possible.

The problem of teachers being overworked could have been avoided by the employment of part-time supply teachers.

Anticipating conflict

Having described some tactics for dealing with unexpected conflicts, for preventing conflict from escalating, and for dealing with conflict-induced stress, let us now explore a number of ways of *forecasting* what kind of resistance we might expect, to action we might want to take! It is always easier to deal with problems if you know in advance what they are likely to be.

Kite-flying

Kite-flying entails presenting a proposal in such a way that it can be disavowed by the presenter if opposition appears to be too strong. For example:

> Aaron was asked to quote a fee as a consultant to write some staff development programmes for a bank. He wanted the consultancy but felt he was in danger of losing it if he quoted too high a figure. He wasn't sure of the extent to which the bank would be prepared to negotiate. Therefore, with the permission of a colleague, he showed the bank's training manager a proposal his colleague had written for a similar training programme, and the fee she had charged. The manager commented immediately: 'Oh, the bank would never pay that much!' Aaron then went away and worked out a simplified proposal that nevertheless incorporated the essential elements required by the bank, and was able to get his fee down to a level that the bank accepted without question.

Distracting the opposition

Every conjuror knows that 'the quickness of the hand deceives the eye'. Sometimes you can avoid opposition by turning the eyes of your potential opponents from the issue that is of real importance to you. Instead, you distract them with matters that are controversial, but irrelevant to your interests. This strategy can also be labelled 'divide and conquer' because it demonstrates that splitting the opposition into factions can be a successful method of getting your own way without involving you in the conflict. For example:

> Jeff had recently interviewed a woman, who happened to be a black woman from Nigeria, for a position in the company. Her application was unsuccessful but Jeff had been struck by her capability and wanted her for his own department. However, he knew that any enlargement of his present staff would meet with considerable opposition from other, power-conscious department heads. He needed to deflect their hostility. Therefore, at their next monthly meeting he raised the issue that the company EEO officer had recently criticised the department's lack of affirmation action programmes. Jeff knew this would infuriate his (all male) colleagues, who felt that the EEO officer (whom they described as 'that wretched woman') was advocating 'reverse discrimination' against themselves. Jeff then offered to appease her by creating a place in his section for a member of a disadvantaged minority group such as a black person – which must be regarded as a highly visible sign of affirmative action. His suggestion was seen by his colleagues to be a brilliant move in the war against the EEO officer, and it was unanimously approved.

Forming committees

This is another version of 'Distracting the Opposition': to avoid problems by distracting potential troublemakers from the main issues by inviting them to form committees to go more deeply into peripheral matters and report back to you. It is a strategy that has something in common also with 'Canvassing' (page 50), except that now others are doing the information-gathering instead of you; and with 'Joining Forces' (page 56) because it has the appearance of collaboration although without the substance.

Information 'leaks'

This is another form of distracting the opposition, often used by power-holders for discreditable purposes, for instance to create distractions so that opponents will spend more time plugging leaks than pursuing policy changes. The following example is of the use of an office 'grapevine' to spread false rumours in order that the truth — which otherwise might be unacceptable — shall appear as a welcome alternative. The ethics of this method are debatable, to say the least; but nonetheless it is used! An example follows:

Jo was a factory department head, about to apply for promotion, who wanted to impress management with her fiscal abilities. She decided to make budget savings by reducing overtime payments for the workers in her department, whose job was to process frozen fish into fish fingers. She anticipated considerable resistance from them to the idea of cutting their overtime money, so she asked Teri, the head of the Technical Division, to give her a copy of a proposal, which she remembered seeing some time ago, to automate the production line 100 per cent, thereby eliminating this team of workers altogether.

Teri reminded her that senior management had already decided to reject this proposal because of the high cost of the changeover. 'Never mind that,' replied Jo. 'All I want is a copy of it.' Teri provided her with a copy of the confidential report, to be read by heads of sections only. Jo removed the dated page which detailed why the proposal had been rejected, and then left the actual proposal, as if by accident, beside the photocopy machine. She knew that at least one of the office staff would read it, and that the news of its contents would spread like wildfire along the department grapevine. Sure enough, a stream of process workers passed through her office, asking if it were true that the firm was considering automating the process section and cutting jobs.

Jo was able to assure everybody, quite truthfully, that the rumour was without foundation, but added that there was the possibility of having to cut overtime. This information was greeted with relief, and the overtime cuts went through without a murmur as being the lesser of two evils.

Lobbying

This includes any behaviour designed to get decision-makers, or those who influence decision-makers, on your side and thus reduce the possibility of conflict before actual negotiations take place.

A community health centre was threatened with closure by the local council. The manager, Phil, knew that he had little hope of influencing the council on his own, since any arguments he could offer would be taken as an effort to save his job. He mounted a campaign to form a Hospital Action Group to monitor health care in general in the area, enlisted the support of several local councillors and the local member of parliament, and the association was formed with Phil as chairman. He persuaded the association, as the first of its activities, to lobby the council to preserve the health centre. His strategy was successful, and the association, flushed with success, went on to become a powerful lobby group for health care in the area.

Canvassing

This covers all information-gathering for the purposes of putting yourself in a more powerful negotiating position. It includes the use of surveys, public opinion polls and other such mechanisms, to assemble a body of data in favour of your cause.

Perry wanted to learn martial arts but classes at the local gym were too expensive. The possibility occurred to him that his company staff development unit (SDU) might agree to run such a course if he could think of a way to persuade them. He surveyed a large number of women in the factory, asking each if she would be interested in a self-defence course, should the SDU decide to run one. The response was very positive, so he wrote a proposal along these lines to the SDU, enclosing the results of his survey. He argued that the comparatively isolated location of the factory – which meant that female employees had to walk some distance to the bus stop, often after dark – warranted a course for women in self-defence. The

SDU agreed to run the course, but since they could not equitably exclude men from it, Perry was also able to learn martial arts.

Advocacy

The most obvious example of advocacy is in law, when clients engage the services of a professional advocate to settle disputes out of court. Another example is that of the boss's secretary, assistant or second-in-command, whose advocacy role is also, in a sense, to 'settle disputes out of court' by dealing with potential trouble before it gets to official levels. The following is yet another example of advocacy in the form of company policy to avoid potential trouble in the workplace by dissuading unsuitable people from applying for employment vacancies.

A large investment company employed a recruitment officer, Sally, who was based on the campus of a local university. Sally's advocacy role was twofold: she was instructed to persuade promising final-year business students to apply for jobs in the company; and to dissuade unsuitable students from applying. One day a final-year student came to see her, expressing a wish to work for her company. His academic record was excellent, he was almost certain to obtain a First Class Honours degree in metallurgy, and the company urgently required new recruits with this background. However, the student was a prominent member of the students' union and outspoken in his attacks on academic management. Sally felt sure his view of industrial relations would quickly make him a thorn in the flesh of her company. Accordingly she informed him, truthfully, that although the starting salary he would command was high (which had attracted him to the company in the first place), promotion to the next rung of the corporate ladder was very slow. What she didn't tell him was that after this initial promotion had been achieved, advancement was rapid and very well rewarded. 'With your brilliant academic and leadership records,' she said, 'You don't want to be stuck for years in a junior position with no authority or control!'

'No, I certainly don't!' replied the young man. 'Thank you for being so frank with me. I'll look around for employment that will suit me better!'

Devil's advocate

Turning a situation around and looking at it from the point of view of the opposition can be very helpful. The following example illustrates one method of doing this.

Margaret lived with her mother who, while being loving and supportive, was her sternest critic. Margaret was contemplating a career change and although she was currently employed as a secretary she was thinking of applying for a vacancy in her company for the position of assistant to the computer training officer. She thought there would be resistance to this idea, but wasn't sure what form it would take, so she ran the idea past her mother, who at once put up all sorts of objections to Margaret's capacity to do the job. Her mother knew nothing about computer training; she based her criticisms on her knowledge of Margaret's character and work experience.

'You haven't got the patience or the training to be a teacher,' she said in part. 'And although you've had a lot of experience with computers, you've never tried to teach anybody else to use them!'

Margaret listened to all this, and used it as preparation for her interview. As a result, she was able to anticipate the kind of objections she would meet, and was able to answer them. She had learned patience, she said, through working as a secretary for a number of bosses (she named one whom everybody present knew was a tyrant). She had no formal teaching qualifications but had taught Sunday School to primary school children for several years. She had considerable knowledge and expertise with computer hardware and software and was looking forward to sharing that knowledge and to gaining more through working with the computer training officer.

She got the job.

Giving a push in the right direction

Obtaining the decision you want is one thing; but implementation of that decision is another. How can you avoid the frustration of delay?

Gail asked for a pay rise, on the grounds that her job had been enlarged. The company agreed but the rise was slow to appear in her pay packet. She mentioned this several times to the pay officer, but always received the same reply: that 'the paperwork hadn't come through'.

It occurred to Gail to refuse to do the extra work that her job enlargement entailed until she got the agreed pay rise; but she felt this would put her in a weak position. Then she remembered that her office was due for one of the company's twice-yearly quality control audits.

She commiserated with her boss that the audit would not be as favourable as previously. 'Why not?' he asked.

'Well,' replied Gail, 'one of the performance criteria is based on good inter-departmental communication, and we don't have that.'

'Yes, we do!' snapped her boss.

'Oh, I'm sorry,' said Gail. 'Maybe the delay in my getting my pay increase is only an isolated case?'

Her boss promptly instigated an enquiry throughout the office and found other cases where his staff's paperwork was slow. Since he wanted a good report from the quality control people he tightened up procedures. Gail got her increase in her next pay packet, and the office was commended for quality in performance.

Face value

Sometimes a possible source of conflict can be 'nipped in the bud' by giving the potential trouble-maker a seemingly important but not critical job. This keeps the person happy and occupied and thus renders them harmless.

The monthly general staff meeting was threatening to become stressful owing to Cathy's behaviour. She was a new filing clerk who genuinely wanted to support Zed, the head of section but, unfortunately, she went about it the wrong way. During meetings she constantly interrupted him or other speakers by such actions as offering to make tea or coffee, or by suggesting she open or close the window, and continually jumping up from her chair to run these helpful errands.

During the first meeting everybody put up with her behaviour, recognising the good intentions behind it; but when Cathy began interrupting the next meeting in the same ways, Zed realised it was time to call a halt or he would have trouble on his hands. Sooner or later somebody would speak sharply to Cathy, who might well burst into tears and there would be a very uncomfortable scene.

So the next time she got up from her chair he said to her, 'Come and sit beside me, Cathy, I need you to take some notes for me.' Cathy was delighted to be so useful and sat quietly writing for the rest of the meeting. In fact, she turned out to be a natural minute-taker and Zed, who had previously taken the minutes himself, was happy to leave it to her in future.

The force of contrast

The classic example of avoiding or reducing conflict by force of contrast is that of police interrogation. A suspect is questioned first by a stern-faced, apparently hostile officer and then left alone for a while. After this, a different officer talks with the suspect much more kindly, maybe offering a cup of tea or a cigarette. Frequently, the suspect is so relieved by this treatment, so good in contrast to that of the first officer, that the interrogation proceeds satisfactorily.

You can apply this technique, for example by sending a delegate to a potentially difficult negotiation, with instructions to take a firm stand on all items on the agenda, including those over which you are willing to make compromises, and to ask for an adjournment when the going gets too tough. When the meeting reconvenes, you attend it yourself and take a much softer line. Frequently, the other parties will be seduced by the contrast into making concessions they might not otherwise have agreed to so easily.

Lightning conductor

'Lightning conductor' is similar in strategy to 'Force of contrast'. Nobody likes disciplinarians and if you have to play this role you risk becoming unpopular with your employees. Therefore, it is useful to have someone on hand who will deflect criticism from you. This is sneakier than having an advocate because it entails appointing somebody on your staff to do a job which you know will make them unpopular.

Blaming the boss

This is a contrasting strategy to 'Lightning conductor' because it operates upwards not downwards. It consists of your disclaiming responsibility in deference to a higher authority. Thus, it is similar to 'Force of contrast' but broader in concept because it allows you, the negotiator, to make contentious decisions and blame the boss for your having to make them!

In some instances, 'blaming the boss' can carry with it an implied threat. Parents often use this tactic with naughty children: 'Just you wait till your father (or mother) comes home!' A more formal version is 'The boss won't like it!'

Sharing the glory

There is a Hollywood story, perhaps apocryphal, that Bing Crosby always refused to allow his name to be the only one given top billing in advertisements for his films because he wanted his fellow actors not only to share the credit but also to share the discredit if the film were a box-office flop. Whether the story is true or not, you will meet with less jealousy and resentment from colleagues if you are generous in acknowledgement of their contribution, and you won't have to carry all the blame if things go wrong!

Going to the top

In case study 5 in Chapter 1 Sally was involved in conflict with a local council employee who refused her a parking permit. Eventually, she wrote to the department manager and obtained her permit but not until she had been reduced to tears by fruitless negotiation with the woman behind the counter. Sally could have avoided a great deal of stress if she had abandoned the argument as soon as she could see it was getting her nowhere and gone 'straight to the top'.

Joining forces
There are times when you can abort opposition by inviting the other side to participate in your decision-making. This is typical behaviour by company managers towards union representatives, and while it doesn't always prevent small conflicts from escalating into big ones, at least it's an attempt at doing so. Also it is arguable that most serious management—employee confrontations are due to long standing poor relations between the parties, rather than a flaw in the concept of 'joining forces'.

Granting concessions
Frequently, you can avoid conflict by granting concessions; but you need to be sure you can afford them. The traditional method of doing this is that of bazaar sellers who quote you an outrageous price for their goods in the expectation that you will bargain them down. In many circumstances, however, this is not a dignified way to do business. A more effective means is to offer a concession in exchange for one from the other party.

Recognising the enemy
This chapter should not end without reference to one more situation where you can prevent small problems from growing *provided you recognise them in the first place*. It is a situation in which you are cast as the villain of the piece!

Some years ago, when equal opportunities legislation was in its infancy, a large and very conservative bank reluctantly employed an EEO officer. The bank made a great show of recruiting a highly qualified and able woman, called Ina. She was told, when appointed, that she would have the title of EEO manager, a handsome salary, her own department, staff and budget.

The reality turned out to be very different from her expectations. Her 'department' consisted of two small, dark rooms at the back of the building, whereas all the other managers had large suites of offices with fine views over the neighbouring park. Her 'staff' consisted of one young woman, a recent school-leaver with minimum skills, and the 'budget' barely covered her and her 'secretary's' salaries. Moreover, when she tried to obtain figures on the number of women employed in the bank, their positions, opportunities for promotion and so on, she met with a resistance that was the worse for being passive.

It was obvious to Ina that the bank was paying the merest lip-service to the law by putting her in a no-win position. The bank could, and did, advertise itself as an equal employment opportunity employer, with the option of blaming her if there was any criticism of the reality, which was in stark contrast to appearances.

Ina did her best with the job for a year, after which she resigned in sheer frustration. It is arguable that she could have avoided the whole situation by being more alert in the first place to the presence of a hidden agenda; and that she should have asked more probing questions before taking on the job.

This case study illustrates the need to develop a kind of 'sixth sense' that tells you when you are being 'set up'. One of the difficulties of recognising such a situation is that obviously your opponents won't volunteer any information you could legitimately be given, if it would be detrimental to their case. And although they cannot refuse to give it to you if you ask, you can't ask questions about something you don't know exists! Moreover, they will probably be adept at spotting any irregularity in your questions.

If Ina, for example, had asked how her terms of employment compared to those of other managers, she would probably have been told that to answer this would be a breach of confidentiality. Therefore, before you accept any offer, in any negotiation, play devil's advocate to those who make it. This advice will become clearer if we role-play the interview that Ina had with the bank before she accepted such a disastrous bargain.

INA	May I ask about your commitment to the principles of equal employment opportunity? For example, what have you done so far to apply them in your bank?
MANAGER	I can assure you there is no discrimination here.
INA	Thank you, but can you tell me how many of your senior managers are women?
MANAGER	I don't have that information to hand.
INA	Will I have access to such information on becoming your EEO manager?
MANAGER	I assume the personnel department would have it.
INA	Would I be certain of your full support in gathering the relevant data?
MANAGER	That would not be my responsibility.
INA	Then who would I be reporting to?
MANAGER	Your position will be a new one, and the chain of command hasn't yet been established.

You can see from this dialogue that Ina by now should be having serious doubts about the bank's commitment. It illustrates the kind of probing questions you need to ask in any situation where there is the remotest possibility that you might end up with 'the dirty end of the stick'!

CHAPTER 4

Negotiation Power Across Gender, Age, Disability, Culture and Nationality

After reading this chapter, you should be able to:

- Discuss special problems in negotiations where one or more of the parties may be disadvantaged because of their gender, age, culture, nationality; or physical or mental state;
- Analyse case studies to identify the confusion many men and women experience in the workforce today in negotiating their professional relationships;
- Identify the disadvantages to women of stereotypical assumptions about the behaviour of women in management compared to that of their male counterparts;
- Recognise that negotiation between men and women will be handicapped by assumptions that women typically behave differently from men;
- Recognise that culturally held beliefs about the respective roles of young people, senior citizens and physically challenged people in society will affect negotiations that concern them;
- Discuss the respective uses of five negotiation 'tools' to empower you in situations where your gender, age, culture or nationality are likely to disadvantage you;

- List a number of 'dos' and 'don'ts' for behaviour in cross-cultural and cross-national negotiation;
- Identify some of the problems of employing people with disabilities, including problems of grievance resolution;
- Identify the advantages of a Processor style of negotiation for negotiators with special problems who want the other party to focus on facts rather than feelings.

The battle of the sexes

Equal employment opportunity and affirmative action in workplace negotiation

Case study 1

A senior manager, an American, insists that he is a strong supporter of equal employment opportunities for women, but he says he doesn't know how to behave to women who achieve management positions.

'I know how to behave to my wife and to the wives of my colleagues,' he says. 'I know how to behave to my daughter and my daughter's female friends. I know how to behave to my secretary. But I have no idea what behaviour is expected of me towards women who are my professional colleagues, peers or seniors. For instance, I often put my arm round a male colleague's shoulders, but I daren't do that to a female colleague. I often ask other male departmental managers out to lunch or to have a drink after work; and we usually discuss mutual concerns over a meal or a drink. But if I were to invite a female manager to join me for a drink after work, she'd think I was making a pass at her.'

Case study 2

Elizabeth is a university lecturer. Recently the Dean of her Faculty asked her to his office to discuss her promotion prospects. When she arrived at his office she asked if she should shut the door, since the corridor outside was quite noisy. The Dean replied she could do so if she wished, but in that case he would ask his secretary to be present throughout the meeting. The inference was clear: that he was on his guard against any possibility that Elizabeth might later complain of sexual harassment. Elizabeth was furious – and got her own back by replying: 'Well, John, if you don't think you can control your animal passions if we are alone together, I think we had better leave the door open!'

Discussion

Both these case studies illustrate the confusion men and women experience in the workforce today over their professional relationships with each other. Moreover, some men feel resentful of 'reverse discrimination' when they think they see high-status, high-income jobs being given on the basis of gender to women less qualified than themselves.

On the other hand, there are many men who welcome women as professional peers and even superiors. Meanwhile there are women in these positions who are confused – after a struggle of decades for equality in the workplace – between traditional views of men as the holders of power and new visions of themselves and their sisters as achievers of power. Yet organisational men and women must learn to negotiate and reconcile these different perspectives to achieve workplace harmony, effective performance and high productivity.

Try the following questionnaire to identify your particular 'hang-ups' in the battle of the sexes!

Questionnaire

1. In *personal* relationships, what really 'bugs' you about the behaviour of members of the opposite sex?

_____

_____

2. In *professional* relationships, what really 'bugs' you about the behaviour of members of the opposite sex?

---

3. What do you respect and admire about members of the opposite sex in personal and professional relationships?

Discussion

If you found more difficulty in answering question 3 than questions 1 and 2, you may also have difficulty in day-to-day negotiations with members of the opposite sex in personal and professional contexts. Let's examine some typical assumptions about the behaviour of women in management compared to that of their male counterparts. Ask yourself honestly how many of these assumptions you share!

1. If a manager's desk is cluttered with papers, correspondence, files, reports and so on:
   HE HAS LOTS OF IMPORTANT WORK ON HAND.
   SHE IS DISORGANISED.

2. If there are family photos on the desk:
   HE IS A DEVOTED HUSBAND AND FATHER.
   SHE ISN'T WHOLEHEARTEDLY COMMITTED TO HER JOB.

3. If a manager forgets an appointment:
   HIS MIND IS PREOCCUPIED WITH MORE IMPORTANT MATTERS.
   SHE IS SCATTERBRAINED.

4. If a manager stops to chat with staff members:
   HE IS FRIENDLY AND APPROACHABLE.
   SHE IS A GOSSIP.

5. If a manager criticises a colleague:
   HE IS ENTITLED TO HIS OWN OPINION.
   SHE IS A BITCH.

6. If a manager expresses support for the problems of a staff member or colleague:
   HE IS GENEROUS, FAIR-MINDED AND CAN SEE MORE THAN ONE POINT OF VIEW.
   SHE IS BEING EMOTIONAL.

7. If a manager expresses concern for employees' feelings and the importance of harmony:
   HE IS HUMANE.
   SHE IS SUPERFICIAL AND FRIVOLOUS.

8. If an employee is openly ambitious and actively seeks promotion:
   HE HAS DRIVE AND AMBITION.
   SHE IS CLAWING OR SLEEPING HER WAY TO THE TOP.

9. If a member of a team or committee doesn't hesitate to speak out and express views and opinions:
   HE IS CONTRIBUTING POSITIVELY TO THE DEBATE.
   SHE IS PUSHY.

10. If there is one woman among six men on a committee:
    SHE IS THE TOKEN FEMALE AND CAN SAFELY BE IGNORED.

11. The following are natural laws:
    (a) As a general rule, the most incompetent man is more all-round efficient than the most competent woman.
    (b) Men are good with tools, equipment, budgets, operations management and decision making (ie all the really important things in life!); women are good with people.
    (c) Men think (ie they are rational beings); women feel (ie they are emotional and therefore unreliable).
    (d) Men want power; women want people to like them.

By identifying the discriminatory nature of polarisations like these, we can see how unfair they are. But is there some substratum of truth behind them? Do women *as negotiators* typically behave differently from men?

Women as negotiators

Read the following examples. After each one, note down your answer to the questions that follow it. Then check your answers in Chapter 6.

Example 1*

Ket Nguyen is a senior from Waipahu High School. Recently Ket completed a science project on papayas; and defended it through a competitive process, first to win top place in a Leeward District contest, and then to represent Hawaii at a summer National Youth Science Camp. Ket was one of the two delegates from Hawaii who joined two delegates from every state in the USA to attend this prestigious four-week programme and will attend the International Science and Engineering Fair with the project.

Questions

1. Is Ket: Male ☐   Female ☐   Don't know ☐
2. What are the reasons for your answer?

_____

_____

_____

_____

* Based on a report in *Downtown Planet Weekly*, Honolulu, Hawaii: week of 31 July 1995: p. 4.

Example 2

Statement by A

I used to tune B out. This employee grated on me. The more I tuned out, the more B would push some point. Finally I said to myself: maybe what B is saying really does make sense. Just because personally I find B offensive doesn't mean B's ideas are poor. So I started listening to B's suggestions for improving our rate of production. Once I got past my negative attitudes, B began to be less abrasive. What I need to do now is help this staff member to see how a desire to be heard and have ideas appreciated can lead to being too pushy and triggering many of the communication problems B has with others.

Questions

1. Is A: Male? ☐   Female? ☐   Don't know ☐
2. Why do you think so?

_____

_____

_____

3. Is B: Male? ☐   Female? ☐   Don't know ☐
4. Why do you think so?

_____

_____

_____

Example 3

Smith was head of a laboratory 'think tank' in an American pharmaceutical company. Smith's senior manager requested that a newcomer, Brown, be included in the team. Smith was told that Brown was a brilliant scientist. Smith agreed that Brown should join the group but became very annoyed when during the first meeting the scientist attended, Brown spoke out contemptuously against the American bias towards teams as ideas-generators. Brown insisted that 'group-think' produced only mediocre ideas and that truly creative advances were made by individuals working very closely with particular problems. Brown proposed to undertake personally a research project which until now had been the responsibility of the team, but which so far had proved impossible to put into operation.

Smith was very much aware that everybody present knew that, as their team leader, Smith was dedicated to the concept of teamwork in problem-solving; and that from now on they would be waiting to see how this conflict would be handled between Smith and Brown.

Smith told Brown privately that any personal input to the research would be welcomed but the project would continue to be the responsibility of the team and would be part of the agenda for the weekly team meetings. Brown agreed enthusiastically that these meetings should continue, but added ominously that they would provide a good opportunity for the scientist's progress reports. As the weeks went by, it became obvious that Brown was using the meetings merely to inform team members of progress on the project and for them to 'rubber-stamp' Brown's investigations.

Since Brown was indeed brilliant, the scientist was able to make a real breakthrough on problems that had been holding up the project. Team members began to treat Brown more and more as the leader of the team and Smith's authority as official leader was becoming eroded.

Smith couldn't find any way to negotiate out of this inferior situation. A complaint to the senior manager was futile; the manager was delighted with Brown's progress of the project. Smith began to look round at other companies for another job.

Questions

1. Is Smith: Male? ☐   Female? ☐   Don't know ☐
2. Why do you think so?

_____

_____

_____

3. Is Brown: Male? ☐   Female? ☐   Don't know ☐
4. Why do you think so?

_____

_____

_____

Now turn to the discussion of the above in Chapter 6.

Negotiation across the 'generation gap'

Depending on your cultural assumptions, you are likely to perceive older people either as old-fashioned fuddy-duddies or as repositories of wisdom and authority. Your perceptions will depend also upon whether the older person is male or female, since in most cultures older men tend to be accorded greater respect than older women. Consider the following two case studies:

Case study 1. The old woman and her students

Dr Jefferson is a 60-year-old female professor of management studies at a British university. A few months ago she was invited to Japan to run some workshops for senior Japanese businessmen on 'negotiating with foreigners'. When she arrived at the Management Institute in Nagoya for the first workshop she was met by a very young woman, apparently a secretary, who proposed to take her to the classroom and introduce her to the students. Jefferson thought the whole situation was unsatisfactory. Here she was, in a Japanese environment where status and hierarchy are extremely important. What kind of respect would the students feel for her if she, already disadvantaged three times over for being old, foreign and a woman, were to be further downgraded for being introduced by a young secretary? Granted, they knew she had excellent qualifications and had been specially invited to direct this course, but would that knowledge outweigh the rest?

To do what she could to balance the situation, she said

tactfully to the secretary that she had not yet had the pleasure of meeting the director of the Institute and felt she should pay her respects to him before meeting the class. The secretary then showed her into the director's office. He rose from his chair, came out from behind his desk and greeted her warmly. After they had talked for a few moments he walked down the corridor with her to the classroom and formally introduced her with a short speech in English, welcoming and thanking her for her presence. He informed the participants of the honour she conferred upon them by being willing to share her expertise in cross-cultural communication.

Thus, her connections were established creditably, and she took further precautions to enhance her position, early in the programme, by describing her background and qualifications, mentioning some internationally known companies where she had run management training programmes in the past. Thus, she assembled her power tools of legitimacy and knowledge (as discussed later in this chapter), adding to them the tools of information, coercion and personality as she went along. She was received from the beginning with respect and attention and finally with affection. The participants made plain, at the end of the course, how much they felt they had gained from it. She was asked to autograph the group photographs and several participants kept in touch with her regularly by E-mail.

Case study 2. The old woman and the sales assistant

Eighty-five-year old Lady Joliffant came from an old and distinguished family, and was an extremely wealthy woman. However, she was eccentric. She dressed like a beggar and, although active, she was almost blind but refused to wear glasses. She had a habit of waving her white stick and then walking confidently across busy road intersections, frequently bringing traffic to a squealing halt. The family usually sent a younger relative to keep an eye on her when she went shopping.

One day, accompanied by a great-niece, she went into a fashionable store to buy a silk scarf. She looked at the baskets of bright scarves on display, picking them over and holding them close to her eyes. Finally, she made her selection but by this time a young assistant had begun to tell her, quite rudely, not to touch the goods and to go away.

'Aunt Dora wants to buy this scarf!' the great-niece said bravely. The assistant replied: 'Don't be such a silly little girl, you can see she can't afford it!', but the niece helped her great-aunt find her cheque book and pen.

Aunt Dora made out the cheque but signed it so wildly, thanks to her poor eyesight, that the assistant refused to accept it. Nearby shoppers began taking great interest in the drama and the great-niece, who was only a teenager, wanted nothing so much as to run away. However, she stood by Aunt Dora and demanded that the assistant fetch the manager.

This turned out to be unnecessary because news had already reached him that this formidable lady was in the store. He knew her to be a titled lady and a valued customer so he hurried to the scene, greeted Aunt Dora respectfully as 'Lady Joliffant', reproved the assistant for lack of service and impatiently instructed her to take the cheque and give a receipt. Several watching shoppers applauded and the assistant was nearly in tears of mortification.

Aunt Dora, oblivious of all by-play, thanked her warmly, nodded to the manager and sailed triumphantly out of the store with the scarf in a gift wrapping and her great-niece in tow.

Discussion

If you analyse these case studies, you can see they have several elements in common. Both describe two problems in negotiation caused by *assumptions about age*:

- That old people (particularly old women) are not worth consideration;
- That young people don't deserve to be listened to with respect.

The case studies make it quite clear that these assumptions are held not only by society at large but by old and young people *about themselves*. In Case 1, the professor took it for granted she would *inevitably* be disadvantaged in the eyes of her students because she was an old woman; and that an introduction by a youngster *must* add to her disadvantage. In Case 2, the young assistant assumed the teenager didn't know what she was talking about *because she was a teenager* — only to be humiliated herself by the manager treating her like a child.

If you sometimes feel that you are disempowered in negotiation because of your age, or any other attribute, aspect of your personality, or lack of status, encourage yourself by referring to six sources of personal power, mentioned in Dr Jefferson's story above, that are at the disposal of all of us, if we know how to gain access to them.

Sources of power

Power is the ability to persuade other people to do what you want, preferably in such a way that they will thank you for the opportunity to do it! Based on research by a number of writers it is argued there are six basic sources from which you can derive negotiation power as an individual and as a team leader.

1. Legitimate power

This stems from the authority conferred on you to act in a power position. The classic example of legitimate power is that of the armed forces, where officers have the ultimate power effectively to command enlisted service people to die.

You will have noted in the first case study how the presence of the college director added to the *legitimacy* of the visiting professor's position. In the second case study, Lady Joliffant's title lent her authority because it carried historical associations of the *legitimate power* of the British aristocracy.

Thus, your legitimate power over individuals and groups depends on the extent to which they see you as having the *right* to respect and authority. This may be because the organisation which you all represent has given you the leadership position; or it may be because members of a group, such as a negotiation team, have elected you their leader by mutual consent. If the other parties to the negotiation see you as the formal leader of the opposition, they too will accord you the same respect.

Therefore, ask yourself, in any situation in which you feel at a disadvantage, how can you increase your *legitimate power*?

2. Connective power

Most of the power that international negotiators have is derived from the fact that they represent large multinational organisations or governments. It appears to be a fact that people in general, no matter what their nationality or culture, tend to obey the directives of higher authorities in organisational settings.

An experiment was conducted at Yale University in the late 1970s whereby 40 male subjects, from different backgrounds, were asked to play the role of 'teacher' and administer electric shocks to 'learners' who gave the wrong answers to given questions. In fact, the experiment was a set-up and actors played the roles of the 'learners' and faked painful responses to the 'electric shocks'. However, the subjects thought the situation was real, and 26 out of the 40 'teachers' continued to obey the instructions of the white-coated, authority-laden laboratory staff. They were willing, on orders, to press a switch that apparently 'shocked' the 'learners' up to 450 volts even though they could see for themselves the apparent pain and finally insensibility, even death, that their actions caused. Therefore, your connection with a higher authority will lend you power, just as Professor Jefferson gained authority through her *connections* with her own university and with the Japanese college, and Aunt Dora through her aristocratic connections.

The 'higher authority' doesn't have to be temporal; it may be spiritual. Some of the world's most charismatic leaders have claimed their authority to be divinely conferred.

What connections can you establish to enhance your authority in negotiation?

3. Coercive power

Basically, this means your power to reward or punish others, by money, praise or blame, force or persuasion, the prospect of promotion or the motivation to serve you because they see your goals as their own. Your coercive power over the other parties in a negotiation depends to a large degree on the extent to which they perceive you can benefit or disadvantage them. Professor Jefferson had very little coercive power in the situation described above, which was why she was so anxious to derive authority from other sources. However, what coercion was open to her, she used, and this is discussed under 'personality' below. Aunt Dora scorns coercion as a power tool, as witnessed by a style of dressing which makes no attempt to persuade others of her worth, but is very forceful when it comes to crossing the road.

You can increase your coercive power by the way you dress, the way you walk, talk, smile and frown.

4. Knowledge
Knowledge is power. If you are perceived by others to know more than they do about the given situation, they are likely to accord you authority. Education, both formal and self-derived, carries power with it. Professor Jefferson had knowledge power that served her well, once her credentials had been established. Aunt Dora's latent knowledge of her own unassailable birth and breeding gave her the power of arrogance.

You can increase your knowledge power through learning and self-confidence.

5. Information
This is not the same as knowledge, although linked to it. You can be as knowledgeable as an encyclopedia but if you can't communicate that knowledge, it will not necessarily empower you. If you can provide others with *information* they want or need, about where to go, what to do, what the constraints and liberties are for them in a particular situation, you have power.

What kind of information can you supply, that others need?

6. Personality

In the last resort this is probably your most powerful tool. If you have *no other source of power* your personality alone can win the day for you. Interestingly, this doesn't necessarily mean you have to have good interpersonal communication and persuasion skills, that you need to adapt your style to the company you keep, or even that you need to *do* anything at all to 'win friends and influence people'.

It is quite possible for you to become a powerful negotiator even if you have no legitimate authority, no important connections, no specialised knowledge, no inside information and no capacity to confer material rewards. Many people with little formal education and no influential backing (at any rate to start with) have achieved high office and gained all the other power tools in the armoury (particularly coercive power) purely on the strength of their personalities: Hitler and Stalin are probably two of the most notorious examples.

On a different scale, a teacher–student relationship is a good example of a situation in which one person is likely to have all six power tools to control others' behaviour – as illustrated in the story of Dr Jefferson in Japan. Teaching is a form of negotiation because the teacher has to negotiate the material that has to be learned with the students who need to learn it.

For instance, if you are an instructor running a computer training program for new recruits in your organisation, you have the *legitimacy* of your instructional role, *connective power* as a representative of the company, and *coercive power* because it will be your decision who passes or fails the course; and you can praise trainees' good work and criticise poor progress. You also have *knowledge*, and *information* based on that knowledge, that trainees wish to acquire. Finally, you have the skills that derive from your *personality* as a teacher.

Negotiating with people from different backgrounds from your own

Behaviour checklist
Cross-cultural and cross-national negotiations are such mine-fields that whole volumes have been written about them — several of which are listed at the end of this book. In particular, we recommend anything written by G. Hofstede. Here we can do no more than offer a checklist of cultural differences that may affect negotiation outcomes.

1. In situations where English is used as an international language by native and non-native speakers, the native speakers will tend to dominate the discussion because usually they have more language fluency. If this is in your favour, fine, but if you or members of your team are at a disadvantage in this respect, use an interpreter.

2. Remember that visible signs of status carry more weight in some cultures than in others because they are taken to be symbols of the importance of the person concerned. In negotiation settings these signs include where people sit, what they wear, and the size and nature of their entourage. In cross-cultural settings, play it safe: dress up for the meeting, take a partner and ask the organiser in advance to seat you both next to somebody important — although you don't phrase your request in those words. For instance, if you have met one of the VIPs before, even under the most trivial circumstances, mention you know this person and would like to sit near them. Of course you may be one of the VIPs yourself, in which case people will want to sit next to you.

   If any of this sounds undignified and scheming, then reflect that this kind of behaviour is to some extent inevitable in any form of bargaining. Public figures pay fortunes to international consultants to tell them how to act in cross-cultural environments.

   We know a woman, a world-travelled public relations director, who used to wear a mink coat to important business meetings in the days when fur coats were fashionable. She said she did so only in order to throw it carelessly over the back of her chair so that it trailed on the ground. She said somebody would always pick it up, or comment to her on the risk of such a gorgeous coat becoming dirty. This drew attention to her as a person so wealthy she could afford to be careless with symbols of wealth. The result was to intimidate many people into thinking she would be a hard person to bargain with.

3. Formal gestures of respect are more important in some cultures than in others. An exchange of business cards, for instance, is an important ritual between Japanese business people. When in doubt, behave formally rather than informally.

4. Modest behaviour is polite behaviour in all cultures.

5. Use of first names may be fine for Americans and Australians; otherwise avoid it unless you are specifically invited to call somebody by their first name.

6. Age differences carry different connotations in different cultures. In Japan, for example, older people are accorded special respect, but Australia is a youth culture. If you are very young or very old (relatively speaking) use your age to your advantage. If you are older than most of the other people present, *take it for granted* that you will be accorded the status of 'elder statesman – or -woman'. If you are younger than most people present, make it clear that your presence there is all the more impressive for your youth.

This evidence may be provided in unexpected ways: on one occasion – an international academic conference – an elderly Japanese scholar was so surprised to meet a young female professor from an American university that he asked, in front of everybody: 'How old are you?' He meant it as a compliment, which it was in his culture; unfortunately, the American construed it according to her own culture and replied: 'None of your damn' business!' The moral of this story is that one should turn everything to one's advantage in alien settings. The woman would have done much better to have answered: 'I am 28 years old, Professor', which would have given him the opportunity (which undoubtedly he would have taken) to praise her in public for achieving so much success, so young.

7. A popular adage is that Japanese begin a speech with an apology, Americans begin with a joke. Jokes are usually culture-specific and people from other cultures often don't find them funny. Unless you are sure of your audience, cut out the funny stuff.

8. Some cultures value interdependence, others independence. If you come from an individualistic culture, as in America, you may appear crass and 'pushy' to Japanese, who instinctively look at each other for support or confirmation before they express any opinion. On the other hand, interdependent behaviour can appear to Americans to lack confidence. British negotiators tend to act as a team, French people as individuals. Italians are inclined to refer to each other, Germans are not, and so on. In these international settings, the safest tactic is to be consultative, not individualistic.

9. Beware of saying 'yes' and 'no' in cross-cultural negotiation. These words are altogether too final in many cultures where people prefer to leave the door open, if only a crack, for exit or entry. Say 'maybe' or 'that sounds difficult (or easy)'; or 'I see no immediate problem' or 'I shall have to ask for direction from my superiors on that one'. Say anything except a straight 'yes' or 'no'.

10. Don't express your personal opinions on anything. It is so easy to give offence if you don't know the cultural context. Instead, say something like: 'I have heard that . . .' or 'Somebody told me that . . .'; or 'I think it is generally accepted that . . .'. If you want to pay somebody a compliment, or an insult, do it indirectly. Don't tell an Englishman: 'That was the greatest speech I ever heard!' He won't know how to respond and he will mark you down as a gushing fool. If you really want to praise him, say something like 'That was quite a good show, don't you think? Everybody spoke well'. If you want to insult

him, say something like: 'I expect you made a good speech, pity I couldn't hear it, I was sitting towards the back of the room' (ie he was inaudible)!

11. Asking too many direct questions is rude in some societies, and members of those societies won't hesitate to answer you with lies because they think you don't deserve any better. If you need information, collect it circuitously, for example during informal conversations, or by background research.

12. Don't come to the point too soon if you are negotiating with people whose customs you don't know. It's better to risk them becoming slightly impatient with your chat about the weather and the crops, rather than offend them seriously by appearing aggressive.

Disabilities and grievances

The following case study illustrates the complexities of negotiating grievances concerning employees with disabilities.

Case study: The suspended teacher

Dennis suffered from a verbal disability – a strong stutter. He was a postgraduate student in the School of Social Science at the University of Culture Risk Management. He had been allocated some part-time teaching by Dr Barnes, the head of the school, to help him financially with his studies. However, a number of the students complained about Dennis's teaching and Dr Barnes suspended him indefinitely, but arranged for him to be given a small scholarship, the equivalent of his part-time teaching salary, so that he would not be financially disadvantaged and unable to continue his studies.

Nonetheless Dennis complained to Lyn, the director of the Equal Opportunity (EO) Unit of the university, that he had been discriminated against on the grounds of his verbal disability. He argued that the students had complained of his teaching because of his stutter, and that he should not have been suspended for this.

Discussion

In fact Dennis's complaint was dealt with fairly easily because Dr Barnes was able to prove that the students' complaints had been of the quality of Dennis's teaching and had nothing to do with his verbal disability. Nevertheless, the case is interesting because it raises some general and complex issues concerning EO in all forms of employment; for example:

1. Students are entitled to the highest standards of teaching *but* should such provision entail refusing to employ teachers who are physically disadvantaged?
2. Packing shoppers' groceries at the supermarket checkout is a job well suited to the capabilities of somebody who is mentally disadvantaged *but* are supermarket managers likely to engage such employees if they think shoppers will become annoyed that their groceries are being packed comparatively slowly?

Negotiations over the employment of disadvantaged members of the workforce – be they women, old people, immigrants, or the mentally and physically challenged – are the concern not just of employers, but of society as a whole. Hence the importance of data collection such as performance appraisals based on the kind of objective methods that are discussed in the following chapter. Thus, evidence can be accumulated to defend your reasons for employing, or not employing, people whose special circumstances may render them controversial as candidates.

Finally, a happy ending to the chapter, with the case study of a very determined woman in a wheelchair.

Case study

James is a manager in a processing plant whose methods have achieved international recognition for innovative thinking. He is considering a candidate, Cynthia, for a position as programme officer. Her duties would be to organise hospitality for visiting delegates who arrive frequently to inspect the plant. The public relations department insists these visitors be treated as honoured guests. Cynthia has good qualifications, speaks several languages, has a pleasant personality and would be ideal for the job – except that she is confined to a wheelchair. James is not opposed on principle to employing people who are physically challenged but he is very doubtful that in this case Cynthia can do the job. She would have to get to the airport, meet the delegates, settle them in their hotel, take them to inspect the plant, and organise a function at which they would meet senior managers of the plant. How can she do all this from a wheelchair? He has asked her to meet him in his office to discuss the problem.*

Now imagine yourself in Cynthia's situation. Spend a few moments thinking of arguments you might use in your negotiation with James over the issue of your being confined to a wheelchair.

SCENE   James's office. James and Cynthia have been talking for a few minutes.

C Let me get this straight. Am I to understand that apart from my being in a wheelchair you would offer me the job?

J Well, there are other applicants. But the fact that you have been shortlisted, in spite of the problem we're now discussing, tells its own story.

C OK, can we agree that if we can get over the wheelchair problem to your satisfaction I would be in a very strong position to be offered the job?

J Yes, that's a fair statement.

(Thus, by rewording James's statements, Cynthia so far has got from him the assurance she needs to continue the negotiation.)

C Can you give me an example of where you think my special circumstances might interfere with the job?

(By asking James to be specific, Cynthia has a better chance of

---

* From Christopher, EM and Smith, LE, *Management Recruitment, Training and Development: A Sourcebook of Activities.*

defending her position. Otherwise she might have to counter vague generalities, which would be more difficult.)

J How can you get to the airport, sometimes at the crack of dawn, to meet visitors to the plant?

C I have a specially adapted car that will take my wheelchair. It's true I need one other person's help to get me in and out of it. When I leave my flat the porter helps me. When I get to somewhere like the airport, or any public place, there is always somebody who is willing to give me the minimal assistance I need.

(Here Cynthia has admitted she has a problem, but immediately describes how she gets over it.)

J Even assuming you can meet the visitors, how are you going to get them to the hotel?

C I would need a small concession from you here. We usually put people up at the Grand Hotel, but that has no wheelchair facilities. If you would be willing for visitors to be accommodated at the Hotel Splendide I would have no problem; there are ramps, big elevators and wide corridors. The Splendide is just as luxurious as the Grand. It's a little further from the plant but the rates are quite a bit cheaper.

(Cynthia has now asked for a concession, but offered one in return, while demonstrating her research abilities.)

J Oh, I can see you've done some homework on this! And it's true you never seem to have any problems getting around within the plant, once you're here?

C I do find the big table in the function room on the top floor is difficult for me to get my wheelchair up to. And when I'm sitting at it, I'm too low. But I notice that some of our Scandinavian and Netherlands visitors, who tend to be big people, also have problems seating themselves; and many of our Asian visitors, who are on the small side, find the table too high for them. Would you consider different seating arrangements in the function room?

(In fact, Cynthia finds it impossible to manœuvre her

wheelchair in the function room because of the awkward table, but she has no intention of telling James this. On the contrary, she finds *other* reasons, that will appeal to James, why the table should be changed. However, she is prepared to admit that she also has a personal stake in this issue.)

J You certainly are observant! And you're very persuasive! I'm very glad we had this talk, Cynthia, it's cleared up a lot of things for me. Obviously I can't tell you definitely that you've got the job till I've talked with a couple of other people, but let's say I look forward very much to working with you.

This dialogue illustrates how the power tools of negotiation – *Legitimacy, Connections, Coercion, Knowledge* and *Personality* — can be used to overcome disadvantages such as Cynthia experienced. She had no *formal authority* in the situation but she acquired a degree of *informal* authority by establishing, from the beginning of the dialogue, her understanding of the issues. Thus, she was able to win some agreement that if she could demonstrate her capability she might get the job. She continued to maintain authority by giving *specific information* about her wheelchair mobility. She indicated her *knowledge* of the circumstances within which she would have to operate (getting to the airport; problems with seating in the function room) and her useful *connections* (for example, with the hotel). Finally, she used her *personality* to impress the manager with her overall efficiency. It is also worth noting that she adopted the negotiation style of a Processor in that her behaviour was as follows:

1. She *planned the negotiation*. In other words, Cynthia did her homework! She found out as much as she could about the job she was being interviewed for.
2. She *anticipated* the kind of objections her interviewer might make to her appointment.
3. She *explored possible concessions*.
4. She *established an agenda* and *negotiated by objectives*.
5. She *negotiated on issues*, not on feelings; and *focused on facts*.

Thus, the style of a Processor can be very effective for you in all negotiations where you are likely to be disadvantaged by bias or prejudice from the other party. Do your homework, plan your agenda and stick to the facts!

CHAPTER 5
People at Work: Employers and Employees

After completing this chapter, you should be able to:

- Conduct effective interviews to select appropriate candidates for employment;
- Argue the pros and cons for a performance appraisal system;
- Identify the essential steps in a performance appraisal system;
- Apply the above steps to investigate apparent lapses in individual workers' on-the-job performance;
- Argue both the employers' and the employees' case in negotiations concerning laying-off workers.

This chapter argues that selection of employees, assessment of their work performance and adjustment to the size of the workforce are the three areas of human resource management that require the most delicate negotiation.

There are other matters for negotiation between employers and employees, such as remuneration, promotion and other benefits; concerns for occupational health, safety and a comfortable work environment, and so on; but most people identify themselves, to a large extent, by the kind of work they do and will be self-motivated to perform tasks that give them satisfaction. Therefore, conflict is most likely to arise between managers and staff in negotiations where outcomes will *directly affect employment and work performance*.

One theorist in this field, Frederick Herzberg, goes so far as to state that an equitable working environment and extrinsic rewards such as payment will not *by themselves* serve as motivators, although employees will become very dissatisfied very quickly if they are not paid adequately or if their working conditions are unsatisfactory. The results of Herzberg's research appear to indicate that recognition, achievement, responsibility and the work itself motivate employees towards high quality performance. If this is so, then any perceived threats in these areas are likely to cause considerable disturbance.

For instance, there are few situations as nerve-racking as job interviews, where candidates are on trial for recognition of their suitability for employment. Also, the sense of achievement and responsibility that employees are entitled to feel for a job well done can be undermined disastrously by insensitive performance appraisal methods, and people will experience real stress if their very jobs are threatened by changes in company fortunes or policy.

For all these reasons, any negotiation over employee selection, performance assessment and 'letting people go' should be handled with skill and sensitivity, not only for the sake of the individuals but for the good of the organisation as a whole.

The selection of suitable employees

Organisations depend on people for their successful operation: hence the need to acquire, develop, stimulate and keep employees who will achieve this success. However, individual and organisational needs are not always in alignment. There is a constant need for negotiation between managers, who have the responsibility for achieving organisational goals through team performance, and the members of those teams who may have their own, apparently conflicting, agendas.

Chapter 3 discussed the importance of *preventing* conflict in the first place, and *containing* conflict when it does occur. A good example of prevention being better than cure is to try to avoid potential conflict between management and employees by recruiting candidates for employment not only on the basis of their actual work qualifications but also for the *quality* of the contribution they are likely to make.

This statement is not an argument that companies should only hire people who will say 'Yes, Sir, No, Sir (or Madam), three bags full', because a workforce needs leaders and innovative thinkers as well as faithful followers. It is a reminder that selection interviews are a form of negotiation that requires the *consenting involvement* of all parties and a *joint settlement* of problems. The object of a selection interview should be to satisfy both parties – employer and employee – that their best interests will be served by working together. If this mutual understanding is clear *from the beginning*, it should serve to contain any future conflict between the parties and prevent it escalating to cause serious damage such as loss of productivity and/or loss of jobs. How, then, to negotiate an interview that will achieve this aim? The following questionnaire should help you towards some answers.

Questionnaire

Q1. Interviewers' evaluations during the interview will be biased according to their previous assessment of candidates' backgrounds (prior information from application forms, test scores, appraisals by other interviewers, etc).

TRUE ☐   FALSE ☐

Q2. Interviewers tend to favour applicants who share their own attitudes and expectations regarding the relevant job.

TRUE ☐   FALSE ☐

Q3. Most interviewers have definite ideas, before the

interview begins, about what does and does not constitute a suitable applicant for the job in question.

TRUE ☐   FALSE ☐

Q4. Interviewers' evaluation of an applicant is likely to be higher if this person's interview follows those of one or more poor candidates; and their evaluation is likely to be lower if this person has been preceded by one or more candidates of high calibre.

TRUE ☐   FALSE ☐

Q5. Interviewers' evaluation is influenced by the style with which applicants provide the panel with information: candidates who present only relevant information, in a methodical way, are likely to be favoured.

TRUE ☐   FALSE ☐

Q6. Interviewers tend to believe that structured and well-organised interviews are more reliable than open-ended ones.

TRUE ☐   FALSE ☐

Q7. Interviewers put a lot of weight on negative information that emerges during the interview, about the applicant.

TRUE ☐   FALSE ☐

Q8. Interviewers tend to make up their minds very early in the interview about a particular applicant's suitability for the job.

TRUE ☐   FALSE ☐

Q9. Interviewers tend to forget much of the content of an interview a few moments after it is over.

TRUE ☐   FALSE ☐

Q10. Interviews are a valid method to determine job-related factors such as applicants' intelligence, level of motivation and interpersonal skills, but not much else.

TRUE ☐   FALSE ☐

Discussion

According to a number of studies the answer to all the above questions is 'True'. If you accept the research findings, then maybe you should consider the following suggestions for increasing the likelihood of hiring compatible people:

1. If prior knowledge of applicants does bias interviewers' evaluations, should they be denied access to candidates' application forms and other background information before they interview the candidate? Perhaps they might thus more effectively assess each candidate's potential value to the company *as a personality* – unhindered by any other considerations? This assessment could then be added to the candidate's file in support or otherwise of the factual information.

   This suggestion has its disadvantages. For example, too heavy reliance on a panel's personal impressions of candidates could result in recommendations based purely on applicants' pleasant personalities, even if some of them are so 'offbeat' they are unlikely ever to fit comfortably into the organisational structure. A collection of individualists, however brilliant, do not make a team, and teamwork is essential to an organisation – but see next item.

2. Preconceptions that candidates should share interviewers' job-related values are based on assumptions about the importance of *a homogeneous workforce*: that if employees, by and large, share and support the values, norms, goals and aspirations of the organisation, then performance and productivity are likely to be high. However, too much homogeneity in organisational settings may inhibit change, even when change might be beneficial. It is,

after all, the grit in an oyster that results in a pearl! Maybe interviewers *should* keep their minds open to the acquisition of creative 'deviants' as well as faithful followers? Perhaps this strategy would result eventually in the acquisition of a workforce whose members, between them, can maintain stability while at the same time promoting necessary organisational change.

3. Should interviewers be warned specifically to avoid preconceived ideas about who would be a 'good' applicant for any particular job? An alternative might be for interviewers to consider the possibility that even if a particular applicant doesn't meet their present requirements for the job, this person might be valuable in other positions. If so, the candidate's name can be kept on file for the organisation's next session of workforce planning.

4. If the order in which applicants are interviewed influences evaluation, should the order be made at random (for example, by drawing candidates' names out of a hat)? This might alert interviewers to the need to assess *all* applicants on their individual merits, no matter in what order they are interviewed.

5. If evaluation is influenced by the style with which applicants provide the panel with information, should they be encouraged to provide interviewers with a wide range of information even if some of it isn't strictly relevant? This suggestion has implications about the kind of questions interviewers ask. For example, a common practice is to ask exactly the same specific questions, put by the same panel members to each candidate. Perhaps a more effective procedure would be to ask more open-ended questions and then listen interpretively to the answers to get a 'big picture' view of all candidates.

6. The above suggestion does not necessarily run counter to the research finding that structured and well-organised interviews are more reliable than open-ended ones. Questions that allow candidates a wide range of reply can be accommodated within the overall structure. This suggestion has implications for item 7.

7. If interviewers put unduly heavy weight on negative information elicited from candidates, perhaps candidates should be given latitude to qualify or amend information that might otherwise appear to detract from their suitability for the job?

8. If interviewers, on the whole, make up their minds about the candidate very early in the interview, maybe this is an argument for reducing the time of each interview? Many panels allow at least half an hour for each, but perhaps 15 minutes would be equally effective and save everybody time, trouble and expense? In the context of items 6 and 7 above, this suggestion implies that fewer questions should be asked, to allow time for more in-depth replies. The suggestion also has implications for item 9.

9. If interviewers tend quickly to forget most of the content of interviews, is there much point in prolonging them? One drawback to this line of argument is that candidates might feel disadvantaged if they were interviewed only for 15 minutes. However, this might be overcome if applicants, when given the time, date and place of interview, were to be informed also of the company policy to restrict all interview times.

10. If interviews only provide a reliable method of assessing applicants' alertness, level of motivation and interpersonal skills, maybe an effective interview should be restricted to questions in these three areas? This might also allow interviewers the opportunity to use interpersonal skills to build some kind of a relationship, however slight and brief, with each candidate; and thus lay the groundwork for future cooperation.

Negotiating awkward questions in interviews

In some countries (for example, Australia, Britain, Canada, New Zealand and the USA) interviewers are forbidden by law to ask questions that do not pertain directly to candidates' competence to do the relevant job. Nevertheless, as an employer you may have some concerns regarding a particular candidate's gender, marital status, age, race or sexual preference. You may feel that one or more of these factors, if present, may lead to future conflict; yet you can't express these doubts openly. How do you get round this problem?

For example, how might you negotiate your way out of the following two awkward situations?

Case study 1. The service station

You are the manager of a large motor service station. You are interviewing candidates for a trainee position as motor mechanic. At present you employ three such trainees, all young men who seem keen on their work, and two fully qualified mechanics, both older men who are happy to guide the youngsters. There is a very comfortable atmosphere in the shop, and it is important that you choose a new trainee who will fit in.

Unfortunately from this point of view, by far the best candidate is a young and very pretty girl. You support the notion of job equality for women and you would like to employ this candidate, but you are well aware of the distraction she would be in this all-male environment.

Can you think of any effective and legal method of bringing the problem into the open so that it can be discussed freely and possible solutions found? When you have made a few notes, turn to Chapter 6.

Notes

_____

_____

_____

Case study 2. The youth club

You are a social worker employed by the local town council. You have just interviewed a candidate for the position of youth leadership training officer with a recreational club for young people. His qualifications are excellent, his personality pleasant and his manner quiet and gentle. He wears an earring, there is a gold chain round his neck and several rings on his fingers.

Theoretically, you would like to hire this man on his qualifications but the job is not an easy one. Many young people who frequent the club are unemployed, angry and frustrated, and some are prone to violence. You have advertised twice for the position of leadership training officer, you have received very few replies, and this man is by far the best candidate as far as qualifications go. However, his experience, although extensive, does not include working with the kind of youngsters he will meet at the club.

You have explained this to him and he is keen to try. Your personal opinion is that the youngsters will assume he is 'gay' and discriminate against him accordingly.

Is there any way you can discuss this with him without giving offence or breaking the law? Make a few notes, then turn to Chapter 6.

Notes

Monitoring employees' performance

Having discussed selection interviews as one of three key topics for negotiation between employers and employees, we now turn to the second, that of performance appraisal.

There are basically three major purposes for a system of

performance assessment: as a basis for rewards and punishments; to identify areas where staff training and development are needed; and as a method of validating staff selection, development and promotion processes.

However, those with experience of industrial relations negotiation are well aware that the topic of performance appraisal (PA) is highly controversial. To help you become a more effective negotiator in this area, here are some of the main arguments managers use for promoting a systematic PA scheme and the counter-arguments by workers' union representatives.* You will see that both sets of arguments are reasonable − which is usually the case in industrial negotiation, and explains why compromise is often so difficult.

1. FOR PA: To be fair to everybody, there should be performance standards right across the organisation, with consistency in assessment of individual and group performance across all levels and departments.

   AGAINST: Consistency across the board is impossible for performance appraisal, since different supervisors are involved and criteria are viewed differently in the various departments.

2. FOR: Supervisors need to monitor workers' performance over time, and provide them with feedback on how they can improve their work.

   AGAINST: A system of once- or twice-a-year PA is not the best way to do this. PA should be a process of day-to-day feedback between supervisors and individual workers, depending on the needs of the job. The company should spend money on training its workforce, not on processing PA forms.

3. FOR: Managers want to identify and characterise poor performance in order to provide appropriate disincentives.

   AGAINST: PAs are counter-productive in this respect because evaluators will refrain from candid comments

---

* Based on Christopher, EM and Smith, LE, *Management Recruitment, Training and Development: A Sourcebook of Activities.*

about poor performance for fear of negative or hostile reactions. A more effective policy would be to alert supervisors to the need to probe for important difficulties or problems that individual workers may be experiencing.

4. FOR: Managers seek to document performance short-comings as evidence of poor performance, should disciplinary action become necessary.

   AGAINST: Although PAs can be useful evidence in defending the organisation against accusations of discrimination and wrongful termination claims, they can be a two-edged weapon. If the PA should have been done and wasn't or was done poorly, it can pose a significant problem for the employer. Moreover, there are more effective methods to document poor performance, such as written memos to workers at the time, with copies in the personnel file.

5. FOR: PA is an effective way to identify workers' special interests and abilities, to help them follow appropriate career paths.

   AGAINST: Good human resource management should include this process without the need for PA.

6. FOR: PA provides a means to recognise and reward outstanding performance.

   AGAINST: PA is not suitable for this purpose. Most PA is based on a grading scale, which doesn't give an accurate picture of employee performance. Statistically, there is 'regression to the mean', ie a bias towards the middle-to-high range which reduces the spread between ratings.

7. FOR: Managers want to tie promotion and remuneration benefits to performance.

   AGAINST: PA is not usually designed to identify original or innovative performance, although it may recognise good hack work and teamwork. Moreover, PA can become very unpopular with staff if it is used to justify remuneration benefits on merit rather than regular pay increases all round.

8. FOR: PA furthers the strategic goals and objectives of the organisation.

AGAINST: PA can be seen by employees as having political overtones, if different criteria are applied at different levels in the organisational hierarchy.

Discussion

In order to achieve a *shared belief* in the possibility of a mutually acceptable compromise, there needs to be a shift in *the degree of power* that each party tries to exert over the other. Both sides need to adopt a less confrontational stand. Such a shift can only take place if the two parties agree on the following four criteria for performance appraisals:

1. *Definition* of specific job criteria against which performance will be measured (ie the establishment of performance *standards*);
2. *Measurement* of past job performance by *comparison* between actual and agreed performance standards;
3. *Justification* of rewards and disciplinary action on the basis of this comparison;
4. *Identification* of appropriate methods to help employees enhance their performance in current jobs and to prepare them for future responsibilities in line with organisational objectives.

These having been established, PA theoretically follows this process:

- Establish performance standards.
- Communicate these expectations to all employees.
- Measure their actual performance.
- Compare it with the standards.
- Discuss the results with the relevant employee.
- Decide what to do next (for instance, to give a bonus, to impose a penalty or deliver a warning, to provide training, to offer promotion).

This sounds fine in theory, but in practice how do you establish work standards so the other steps can follow? It's easy to fall into a trap of your own making by setting and communicating inappropriate goals. For example:

Arun is the public relations manager in a large department store. Like all such stores, it receives a fair number of written complaints, and Arun has appointed a member of his staff, Julia, to reply to them. His objective was to placate complainants. Accordingly, he gave Julia guidelines to follow, depending on the nature of the complaint. Unfortunately, he told her that her performance would be appraised on the number of letters she answered. Julia was a careful and conscientious employee but in order to satisfy Arun she concentrated on the quantity, rather than quality, of replies, and became angry and frustrated when later Arun criticised her for lack of individual attention to correspondents.

Discussion

Arun gave Julia the impression he would use only a *statistical* method of assessing her work, ie number of letters written. He might have avoided the resulting clash with her if he had supported his appraisal with other measures such as *personal observation* (in which case he would have seen for himself that she was a conscientious worker), *oral reports* (for example, telephoning a sample of customers as a follow-up to the letters, to find out if they were now satisfied) and *written reports* (perhaps as part of a peer review by other members of the department). An assembly of data from these different sources makes for much stronger evidence than from a single source, and is more likely to be in line with the appraiser's overall goals for performance.

Nevertheless, it is always difficult to take somebody to task over such a sensitive matter as the performance of their work. Thus, there are three approaches to performance assessment: through the application of *absolute standards* (which means that candidates are not compared with each other, but with the agreed *standard of performance for the job*); an appraisal of the *relative standard* of an individual's work (in comparison with the agreed standard); and reference to the *organisational objectives* that the job relates to.

However, absolute standards are often hard to relate to

people's actual work performance. The usual methods for doing so include peer assessments and supervisors' written reports, checklists or critical incident appraisals of behaviour that – according to the supervisor – make the difference between doing a job well and doing it badly. The major disadvantage to all these methods is their unavoidable element of subjectivity. Fellow-workers are likely to be biased for or against the person under appraisal; and although supervisors are tacitly assumed to be neutral, they are not always so. The proposition has already been discussed that when conflict arises between people, there is never one single source of conflict, and nobody who is involved in it in any way can be neutral. Who can tell what hidden agendas supervisors have, when they submit appraisals of team members' contributions?

The fact that all assessment is essentially subjective can be illustrated by the case of university lecturers grading students' written essays. There are rigid absolute standards for what constitutes an academic paper. These standards relate to structure, evidence of research, logical development of argument and so on: but what does 'evidence of research' mean, for example? One lecturer may give weight to the student having made a number of references, in the essay, to the literature in the field; but another lecturer may not be so concerned with the number of citations as with the form in which they are made. Also, what is a 'logical argument' to one lecturer may appear illogical to another. The length of the essay is also subject to individual interpretation: some lecturers are unconcerned if an essay contains a few hundred words more than stipulated; another will literally count the words and penalise essays that go over the limit, and so on.

Nevertheless, in spite of all the apparently irreconcilable problems in trying to assess quality and quantity of work, performance appraisal systems work satisfactorily in many organisations. Discussion of the following case study may help to explain how this can happen

Case study: What went wrong?
The story so far ...

Billi lived with her mother, an old lady in frail health. Normally, the district nurse called daily to help Billi get her mother dressed and give her breakfast before Billi went to work. However, one week the nurse was sick and Billi had to manage on her own. The result was that for four mornings in a row she missed her usual train, was late for work, and missed part of her shift. On the Friday her supervisor, Jack, called her into his office and gave her a big lecture on punctuality. Jack reproached her for 'letting the others down' because they had to do her work to meet production deadlines, which were predicated on a set number of total working hours for the whole team. He demanded: 'What have you got to say for yourself?', to which poor Billi could only whisper miserably: 'Nothing.' His response was: 'What's wrong with you, Billi? You used to be such a reliable person!'

Jack was a big man, usually good-humoured but inclined to 'fly off the handle', and with a deep voice and a loud personality. Billi was a small, shy, quietly spoken woman. She was overwhelmed by his tirade, burst into tears and gave in her notice — which was the last thing either she or Jack wanted.

What went wrong? Answer the following questions by making some suggestions on how Billi and Jack might renegotiate their conflict on the bases of agreement over *absolute standards*, *relative standards* and *organisational objectives*:

(a) What was the relevant *absolute standard* of performance on which Jack should have obtained Billi's agreement before he took her to task?

(b) What should Jack have done before he criticised Billi for the apparent difference between her *relative standard* of performance and the agreed *absolute standard*?

(c) How might Jack help Billi to play her role in future to achieve *organisational objectives*?

_____

_____

Discussion

To answer the questions above, you needed to recall the steps in the process of performance appraisal, set out on page 94. Thus, in answer to Question (a), the absolute standard for the job was a set number of hours of work by each team member, to achieve a production deadline calculated on that basis. Jack didn't even attempt to confirm that Billi was aware of this. Admittedly, he might have assumed she would know she had to be on time for work each morning, but did she understand *why* her punctuality was so important?

If this had never been explained to her, the responsibility would not be entirely hers that production deadlines might be threatened by her lateness on the shift. Jack should make a note to send a written memo to all relevant employees – including Billi – to inform them of the position. He might also consider a training programme for all the relevant workers, to reinforce organisational objectives and promote motivation and team spirit. Meanwhile, he can only explain the situation to Billi and ask her to pay more attention to punctuality in future.

However, let us assume that Billi did understand the need for her to work her full shift (ie she was aware of the *absolute standard* for the job) and that she agreed that *relatively* her performance didn't measure up to it because she had missed part of her shift four mornings in a row. This comparison having been made, and the gap established, Jack should then have *discussed the results* with Billi.

If he had done so, he would have discovered quite quickly that poor Billi had been late through no fault of her own. Her unpunctuality was not a discipline matter at all. So how could Jack have helped Billi most effectively, in the circumstances, to play her role in *achieving organisational objectives*?

One way might be to change her to a later shift so she

would have more time to help her mother in the mornings. Another might be to take up some of the slack that should be allowed in any plan for operations management. For example, production deadlines might have been calculated on the basis of 80 worker-hours per day (ie 8 hours' work a day by 10 workers) but in fact 11 workers were on the team, in case of setbacks. If that were so, then Jack could afford to give Billi permission to arrive late until her mother's nurse could resume her duties. However, Jack should take the precaution to explain the situation, in general terms, to the other team members, so there would be no resentment at what might otherwise seem inequitable behaviour on his part.

Adjusting the size of the workforce

The final section in this chapter concerns negotiation to reconcile conflict between worker representatives and employers over the threat of workers losing their jobs. For most people the work they do means more to them than just the money they earn by doing it. Involuntary unemployment not only impoverishes but also demoralises them. Therefore, negotiation over potential job losses is fraught with emotional as well as practical overtones. Bear this in mind when you read the following case study, of a threat to close a factory and put all its employees out of work. Then answer the question that follows it. When you have done so, turn to the discussion in Chapter 6.

Brightrose Corporation: A wilting flower?

Brightrose is a factory situated in a small town. It has not been doing well recently and there are rumours that the owners are thinking of closing it down and relocating. Sally is the union representative and deeply concerned because the factory employs many local people who would have virtually no hope of finding other employment. She has sought an interview with the managing director, Tony.

She began by pointing out the threat to the town if the

> factory were to close, but was disconcerted when Tony replied that according to the Personnel Office the factory currently provides employment for only 15 per cent of the adult workforce in the town.

Now Sally has shifted her ground and the negotiation proceeds as follows:

SALLY: I understand that management has become concerned about the cost-effectiveness of keeping this factory open; but why not step up the process of multi-skilling employees to increase factory efficiency?

TONY: Yes, I am aware that Brightrose has a factory-wide multi-skilling programme as a result of our recent agreement with the union. It was designed to give greater job opportunities to more workers, and more job satisfaction. The programme has been expensive and unfortunately it has not had the effect we hoped, of increasing performance to economically acceptable levels. There seems no point in enlarging the programme any further.

SALLY: Well, what other efforts is management prepared to make? The union takes the position that lack of planning at management level has brought us all to this crisis. To put all the responsibility on to the workers to save the situation doesn't seem fair.

TONY: On the contrary, Brightrose has always responded positively to workers' efforts. I call your attention to our actions in Bakerville where, as you know, we also have a factory. Thanks to successful employer–employee relations it has done very well. We recently enlarged it and employed more people. We aim to employ another 250 people there over the next 12 months, which will represent an additional 2.5 per cent of Bakerville's adult workers.

SALLY: The two cases aren't necessarily the same. We suggest that your planning in this factory has not been as good as in Bakerville under a different general manager.

TONY: On the contrary, management here has planned very carefully to try to avoid the present situation. Our multi-skilling programme is an example because it has equipped workers for a possible transfer to other jobs.

SALLY: You are avoiding my point that management is as much to blame as workers for the financial down-turn; and you don't seem to be making any allowances for the effect this crisis is having on employee morale. I suggest that productivity will improve if some of the stress is taken off our shoulders; and the most effective way of doing so is to guarantee all jobs for an agreed period.

TONY: Because of the present financial crisis, management is not in a position to guarantee anything, including your job and mine. If redundancies *must* occur – but I am not in a position to say that they will – we will consult the union to find ways of treating employees as fairly as possible to reduce suffering as much as we can while protecting the company's interests.

SALLY: Not only the workers but all stakeholders will suffer if Brightrose closes this factory – employees, managers, owners, investors, and the local townspeople. Rather than face such a total disaster, wouldn't it be more practical for workers and managers to sit down together and devise an alternative strategy? Isn't it about time you stopped thinking about your work-force as a liability and began to consider it as your biggest asset? We maintain that lack of consultation between employers and employees has got us all into this crisis; but it's not too late to survive it, if you will let us help you.

TONY: I am willing to arrange a meeting between management and workers along the lines you suggest. But I must insist that any such joint problem-solving would have to include discussion of cost-saving measures such as cutting back on overtime and the provision of more part-time and temporary work. Another possibility might be to offer all employees the choice of accepting a cut of, say, 10 per cent in their salaries all round, rather than seeing their colleagues retrenched.

SALLY: If we should accept these measures, which will substantially reduce your losses, we would expect management in return to guarantee people's jobs for an agreed period; and we would expect suitable compensation if, after all our efforts, management in the end should decide to close the factory as a result of their own inefficiency.

TONY: Since I have already explained we are not in a position to guarantee anybody's job, I have to accept your refusal of my offer.

Question

How should Sally respond to Tony's statement? Write a few more lines of dialogue that might re-open the negotiation and lay the foundation for a joint strategy to save the factory. Then turn to the discussion in Chapter 6.

_____

_____

_____

CHAPTER 6
Commentary on Case Studies and Exercises

Chapter 1: Case studies to illustrate individual negotiation styles

Arguably, case studies 1 and 2 both illustrate an Innovator style of negotiation that displays big thinking and envisions broad perspectives. It is a relatively impersonal style that is able to separate the people from the problem. People who own this style tend to negotiate by incorporating many ideas into a new kind of synthesis, often highly innovative: thus providing new options for mutual gain.

Case study 1. The Salk vaccine (page 16)
Dr Jonas Salk demonstrated *big thinking* and *broad perspectives* in his innovative work to develop the first polio vaccine. At the University of Pittsburgh in the 1950s he faced criticism of, and resistance to, his ideas *but he didn't take this opposition personally*. Rather, he worked with his doubting colleagues to overcome their resistance: thus, he was able to *separate the people from the problem*. He *incorporated the results of his own and others' research* and went on to *generate new options* in place of more traditional research methods, and thereby *creatively*

developed an effective vaccine by the use of killed virus. The result was one of *mutual gain* when the vaccine was officially given the go-ahead and the polio toll plummeted.

Case study 2. Western Power (page 16)

Electricity supplier Western Power needed to cut off the electricity for a short period on the 66,000 volt feed line that runs through the Australian NSW country town of Coonamble. The plan was to cut the supply on 24 June 1995. However, one of the technicians *withheld judgement* that this was necessarily *the 'one best answer'*. He viewed the problem from *a broader perspective* and pointed out that the proposal would prevent everybody in the small town from watching the Rugby World Cup Final. He *didn't take it personally* when his senior manager became defensive but instead *he worked with the manager for mutual gain* by proposing that everybody would benefit if Western Power were to install a generator – *an imaginative use of power* – in the well-patronised Coonamble pub, so that virtually the whole town could follow the game.

It was argued that case studies 3 and 4 illustrate a Communicator style of negotiation. Communicators tend to think of negotiation in terms of human relationships, in which the form of the negotiation is as important as the content, including symbolic forms such as badges of office. Human feelings are legitimate, indeed essential, ingredients in the debate. Teamwork is valued, and the establishment of a wide power base. Note that case study 3 is an example of the relative ease with which people can adopt negotiation styles other than their preferred INS, depending on the circumstances.

Case study 3. The union rep and the works manager (page 17)

The union representative, Stephen, appears to be the kind of person who *doesn't like to enter directly into a negotiation*. He seems to need *time to create sociability, to build a relationship*. On the other hand, the works supervisor, John, appears to be more of a Processor and an Activator (see below), in that he likes written notice of proposals and then to come straight to the point when they are being discussed. Therefore, it is not surprising that Stephen would *become frustrated and show impatience* with Jack's less people-oriented style. However, Jack was willing to modify his style and adopt a more friendly approach. His invitation to Stephen to sit down and have a cup of tea was *a symbolic statement* that demonstrated awareness of him *as a human being*. Stephen became aware that now *his emotions were being recognised as legitimate* and he became more amiable. The results were that *a wider power base* was established, with *teamwork* between the two representatives.

Case study 4. Lethal weapons (page 18)
This study of Communicator-style negotiation describes a dispute between chief constables and police officers in Britain in 1995. It illustrates how the police officers were *given a stake in the outcome* of whether or not they were to carry arms on a routine basis. Membership of the Police Federation gave the dissenting officers *a wide power base* from which to express their dissatisfaction with the original proposal, and to show *a united front*. They were able *legitimately to demonstrate their feelings*. The result was *teamwork* by all concerned, with a focus towards an increase in specialist armed units instead of routinely arming patrolling officers.

It was argued that case studies 5 and 6 illustrate a Processor style of negotiation, that follows a planned and logical course of action based on rules and facts. It is the most impersonal of all the styles and least susceptible to outside pressures such as time constraints. Processors tend to restrict their own authority, relying more on agreed agendas and written proposals. You will see how this style in negotiation can be particularly obstructive (case study 5) or constructive (case study 6), depending on how it is applied.

Case study 5. The parking permit (page 18)
In this story of Sally, who wanted a parking permit, the local

government official *stuck to her agenda* that Sally should provide proof of residency in *the specified form* of a gas, electricity or telephone bill. The woman *resisted the time pressure* that Sally tried to impose on her to keep the negotiation short (Sally was on her lunch break) and insisted on the *precedent*, that *rules were rules* and in this case the relevant rules specified the production of a bill. She indignantly denied any *personal involvement* in the matter, even when Sally was reduced to tears and another official took her part. The woman remained adamant *that she had no authority to* change the rules and *referred Sally to a higher authority* to whom she should *apply in writing*.

Case study 6. Marathon run (page 19)

Fourteen-year-old Peter Molloy *negotiated by objectives* when he wanted his family to run with him in the marathon. He *planned the negotiation* carefully by *getting the relevant facts and statistics* and then concentrated his arguments on *issues* rather than the *personalities* of family members. He dealt *factually, not emotionally*, with their various counter-arguments, including their claim that *time pressure* prevented them from getting fit enough to run. Finally, they all joined him, and enjoyed the event.

It was argued that case studies 7 and 8 illustrate an Activator style of negotiation. People who adopt this style are frequently referred to as 'business-like'. They tend to speak clearly and factually, to ask questions and to listen attentively to answers in order to interpret nuances of meaning. They share with Innovators a preference for relying on their own inventiveness rather than deferring to higher authorities. They resemble Processors in their liking for facts and figures but are inclined to be much more flexible in that they take into account the particular circumstances, personalities, location and environment of the negotiation; and they usually have a 'Plan B' in reserve. They don't make excuses for problems, but apply objective standards of problem-solving. They are willing to make small concessions, but usually only in return for larger ones; and they share with Communicators a liking for symbolic forms, such as forms of agreement.

Case study 7. The rented van (page 20)

Hassan was very *business-like* when he rented a van to the woman in the case study. He explained carefully *the terms of the agreement* and when he *listened attentively* to her responses *he relied on his own good judgement* in deciding she might not be a reliable driver. He *took all known circumstances into account* to safeguard the transaction, but his *'Plan B'* was to book a tentative date for the van to go to a panel-beater. When a repair became necessary, he *gave the customer a discount in exchange for cash payment*.

Case study 8. The TV episode (page 21)

Karl *asked questions* to find out why the TV producers objected to the proposed episode in the new series. He *explained clearly his intentions* for the episode and offered a small role change *as a concession* to their concerns *in exchange for* their consent. Finally, his *knowledge of the total environment of TV series production* gave him the credibility he needed to win his case.

Chapter 2: Talking and Listening

The Planning Committee: Some practical suggestions.

Eliminate as far as possible all distractions before the discussion begins. This is not only to 'play for time' but to sharpen your concentration. Examples: If your mouth is dry, ask for a glass of water. If you are too hot or too cold, open or close a window.

If you can't see or hear everybody perfectly, move your position. If you feel yourself becoming stressed, take a few deep breaths and consciously relax your body. If you are tempted to become distracted with irrelevant thoughts – such as personal problems or the amount of work waiting on your desk – put them out of your mind.

If you don't understand something that's said, insist on clarification. Ask questions, seek explanations. Don't adopt a fixed position in the debate, it will interfere with your listening skills.

Take notes. Effective notetaking is a powerful adjunct to listening, so grab your notebook and jot down headings as the discussion proceeds. Write comments against each heading as they occur to you. Use your notes to challenge the motives of your opponents, the relevance of their opinions, the logic of their arguments, the sources of their information and the strength of their evidence.

Be wiser next time and refuse to 'stand in' for a colleague if you haven't been properly briefed.

Chapter 3: Handling Conflict in Negotiation

Double booking (page 39)
If you preferred ending (A) you indicated a preference for the negotiation style of an Innovator. For example, John was more interested in finding out why the mistake happened than in blaming anybody for it. He encouraged Kim to explain the whole picture, to give him a broad perspective on the problem, including what might have seemed to some people to be irrelevant details about the drinking habits of the Primrose Club. He wandered about the hotel to get a picture of that also. Thus, he looked at the problem from a number of angles without hurrying to reach a possibly premature decision. On the basis of a large quantity of varied information, John was able to offer an innovative solution which satisfied all parties.

Note that an Innovative negotiation style is essentially *individualistic*. It has no bottom line, being based on personal observation of the particular circumstances and internal reflection on implications and possibilities; and a desire to find a mutually beneficial compromise. It is also a relatively impersonal style, based on problem-spotting and solving rather than feelings and emotions. The disadvantage of this negotiation style, carried to excess, is that Innovators can become distracted easily. They may lose sight of the end-product – the negotiation goal – because they become so involved in the intellectual pleasure of the negotiation process itself, of exploring possibilities and generating new kinds of options. John was in danger of forgetting that the whole objective of his negotiation was a meeting with his business colleagues; hence the importance of balancing this style with behaviour more typical of Communicators, Processors and Activators.

However, you may have indicated a preference for ending (B), in which case you have indicated a preference for the negotiation style of a Communicator.

In this second version of 'Double Booking', John's frank expression of his feelings is typical of a Communicator style – which is to 'let off steam' and then to be disconcerted when others take these hot-headed comments personally. Fortunately, Kim also seems to own a Communicator style because she is quick to forgive John's outbursts, although she responds angrily to him at first. Both Kim and John appear to value good working relationships and both seem able to use these relationships to advantage.

Communicators sometimes can be perceived by others as impatient, emotional and over-reactive. Hence the importance of balancing this style with behaviour more typical of Innovators, Processors and Activators. However, you may have indicated a preference for ending (C), in which case you have indicated a preference for the negotiation style of a Processor.

In this ending John anticipated Kim's resistance and broke it down by reference to facts, laws and precedents. He based his negotiation technique on specific objectives and then began to look for possible concessions on Kim's part. This is a strategy that is not designed to win friends but rather to influence people. He got what he wanted, but alienated Kim in the process. However, John was not interested in forming a sound, long-term working relationship with Kim. He had already made up his mind she was unreliable – which is almost the worst sin in the book as far as Processors are concerned.

A Processor style leans towards careful planning and can become unbalanced if people's feelings are not included. Thus, a Processor style needs to be balanced by behaviour more typical of Innovators, who look for *mutual* benefits from negotiation; of Communicators, who value human relationships; and of Activators, who look for pragmatic, rather than theoretically sound, solutions.

However, you may have indicated a preference for ending (D), in which case you have indicated a preference for the negotiation style of an Activator.

An Activator style is action-oriented. When negotiators adopt this no-nonsense approach they sum up the situation quickly and act decisively on their own initiative – as did John when he found a speedy solution to the problem of where to hold his meeting. John was also quick to ask for a *quid pro quo* – a concession from Kim in exchange for his having to make new arrangements at short notice. An Activator style is crisis-oriented; Activators become accustomed to 'thinking on their feet'; they can almost always think of a 'Plan B' in an emergency! And, finally, John's business-like response to the situation motivated Kim to be more business-like herself in future.

Summary

In negotiation, people may perceive an Activator style to be headstrong, hasty and prone to bad judgement; an Innovator style to be too discursive and prone to go off at apparently irrelevant tangents; a Communicator style to be too emotional; and a Processor style to be over-particular about rules and precedents. Hence the importance of balancing the four styles of behaviour in negotiation.

Teachers hit by stress toll
Suggestions for answers to question 1 (page 45)

(a) Long periods of maintenance work on buildings.
(b) Communication problems due to the school being split into two sites.
(c) Introduction of new teachers with different values and teaching methods from those of existing staff.
(d) Fluctuating student population, with transient students

feeling unsettled and teachers finding it difficult to assess their educational levels.

(e) Teachers being overworked because many of their colleagues are away on sick leave.

Suggestions for answers to question 2 (page 45)

(a) Setting priorities for maintenance work on buildings, so the work could be organised to cause as little disruption as possible to the normal life of the school.

(b) Changing the organisational structure of the school to accommodate it being split into two sites. Small, semi-autonomous teams might be the answer, each team to be located on the same site, each consisting of a mixture of teaching and administrative staff members.

(c) An orientation programme for new teachers to integrate their values and methods with those in the school.

(d) The employment of specialist staff to assess the needs of short-term, transient students.

(e) More provision for part-time supply teachers in case of shortages in regular staff numbers.

Chapter 4: Negotiating Power Across Gender, Age, Disability, Culture and Nationality

Women as negotiators
Example 1 (page 64). This newspaper report of Ket Nguyen's success makes it clear that she is a female student. If you answered that she was probably male, you may have been misled by the fact she had won recognition for a science project. If you think there is something out of the ordinary about women as scientists, you may be at a disadvantage in negotiations that involve them!

Example 2 (page 65). In the original text on which this example is based, A was male and B was female. However, there is no evidence – direct or indirect – to indicate this in the above version. In real life both men and women may appear aggressive when they try hard to enthuse others with their ideas yet have poor communication skills. And both men and women sometimes find it difficult to listen attentively to people whose manner or attitude they personally dislike.

The lessons from this example are to avoid stereotypical thinking about male versus female behaviour in the workplace and to concentrate on improving one's own communication skills.

Example 3 (page 65). Socialised assumptions about gender lead many people to think of 'managers' and 'scientists' as men rather than women. On this assumption you may have been tempted to answer that Smith and Brown were male.

On the other hand, assumptions about 'women managers' are that they are less eager than men to seek power, and less able or willing to engage in conflict over power roles. Therefore, you may have thought of Smith as female, since apparently 'she' didn't know how to maintain her authority, and Brown as male, since 'he' emerged as a leader able to wrest power from 'her' as the appointed head of the team.

However, to refute this assumption we only have to think of Margaret Thatcher who achieved and maintained power as Prime Minister of Great Britain for ten years. Even if you want to argue that she is an exception to the rule, there are nowadays so many women power-holders at every level in organisational life, both in the private and public sectors, that your argument would be very difficult to sustain.

All one can say is that *some men* and *some women* seek organisational power. Other men and women do not. Therefore, there is nothing in the story *per se* to indicate whether Smith and Brown are male or female.

Chapter 5: People at Work: Employers and Employees

Negotiating awkward questions in interviews: case studies 1 and 2.

Both examples are of situations where negotiation is full of legal pitfalls; and both illustrate the advantages in difficult negotiations of the consenting involvement with others for a joint settlement of the outcome.

Case study 1. The service station (page 90)

If you were the manager of the service station you might ask the candidate to attend a second interview at which the two supervisors would be present with you, together with their three trainees. The interview would cover much the same ground as on the first occasion and you would ensure that the candidate's excellent qualifications for the job were fully recognised.

Then you might convene an in-house meeting between yourself, the mechanics and trainees, during which you could all discuss frankly any personal problems they might experience in working with the candidate. This would give you the opportunity both to gauge the extent of the problem and to make it clear that the men's response to it will be the critical factor in your decision whether or not to employ the candidate.

The men are likely to reply in one of two ways. Either they will provide you with a group assurance that the candidate will be given equal employment opportunity with the male trainees; or they will indicate that they do not think this will be possible.

If they agree to treat the female trainee as 'one of themselves', they will probably abide by this corporate decision and you can go ahead and hire her, but if all the signs point to future distraction and disruption in the workplace, you would do better not to employ her and you will have to think of some reasonable and legal grounds for refusing to do so.

However, at least you will have been able to make it clear to supervisors and trainees alike that their attitude has not only destroyed this girl's career prospects but has also seriously disadvantaged the business and therefore may well damage the security of their own jobs.

Thus, even if this particular candidate has been disadvantaged unfairly, you have increased the possibility that female candidates in the future may receive more equitable treatment from your company. You can increase this likelihood by consulting an equal employment opportunity officer from the relevant government department, for advice on how to handle such problems.

Case study 2. The youth club (page 91)

If you were the social worker who interviewed the candidate for the job of youth leadership training officer, you might follow the same strategy as for case study 1. You might ask several young people from the youth club to meet him for a second interview.

Then later, privately, you could discuss his application with the club members. Your doubts may turn out to be groundless because you credited the youngsters with much less tolerance than they are prepared to extend to the candidate. They may in fact find him to be 'on their wavelength'.

On the other hand, they may respond, for example, that he didn't impress them as the sort of man they could confide their problems to, or who would understand them if they did. In that case you could reject his application on the grounds of inappropriate communication skills.

Whatever the outcome, in a situation such as this, it is advisable for all candidates to meet the young people with whom they will be working if they get the job.

Case study 3. Brightrose Corporation: a wilting flower? (page 99)

Unfortunately, this case study appears to demonstrate the near impossibility of negotiators reaching agreement when their objectives are virtually irreconcilable. However, if we analyse briefly the negotiation between Sally and Tony we may be able to suggest a strategy for conciliation.

1. Sally started off on the wrong foot by not checking her facts. Thus, Tony was able to refute her contention that a large percentage of townspeople were employed in the factory.

2. At this early stage of the negotiation, Sally might have done better to seek Tony's agreement that no matter what percentage of the town's workforce was employed, the general effect on the town of a closure of the factory would be detrimental to everybody. If she had negotiated along these lines, she might have established a less adversarial climate from the beginning.

    As it was, she went on the attack by demanding more multi-skilling. Tony defended the management position by pointing to the failure of the existing programme – a failure that Sally would be aware of, therefore her attack was weak from the start.

3. She attacked again, by accusing the factory management of incompetence and arguing that therefore it was management's responsibility to solve its problems without penalising the workers.

    Tony then made a mistake by quoting management's success in another factory, which gave Sally the opportunity to expose his lack of logic. This annoyed Tony, who then became adversarial in turn, by implying it was the fault of the workers, not of management, that the multi-skilling programme hadn't worked.

4. Nevertheless, Sally senses she is on a temporary winning streak over the issue of management incompetence, and pursues it to try to obtain the concession that workers' jobs should be guaranteed. She was unwise at this stage to press for a yes-no answer because she gave Tony the opportunity to say no.

5. Sally abandons what is obviously a lost cause and reverts to her earlier argument, that everybody will suffer if the factory should close. However, again she 'rushes her fences' by asking for joint consultation between workers and managers to help resolve the financial crisis.

6. Although Tony is willing to discuss this possibility, he indicates clearly that the agenda for any such joint meeting would contain only items relating to cutbacks in workers' remuneration packages.

    At this point Sally might have done better not to press

for further concessions but instead agree to a meeting whose agenda, by implication, would not include a proposal to close the factory – which would be the ultimate disaster.

By demanding a guarantee of all workers' jobs in exchange for her agreement to the meeting, she lost her case. Tony is now in a position to claim, correctly, that management had offered a general meeting with all employees to explore alternatives to closing the factory but the union had refused to cooperate. Management can use this as an excuse to go ahead with whatever plans they have.

How can Sally retrieve her position? Remember you were asked to bear in mind, when you studied this case, that any negotiation over potential job losses has strong emotional connotations. Therein lies Sally's best strategy. If she were to revert to her original argument, that it is in *nobody's* best interests to throw a large proportion of the townsfolk out of work, she might be back in the game.

Deep in the culture of all post-industrialised, capitalist-based societies is the belief that everybody has a right to work. Tony represents an organisation that is part of that culture. In the face of every economic argument to close the factory, senior management is likely to consider such a drastic measure only in the last resort – or what they can claim is the last resort – if only to avoid public censure for being a harsh employer and political criticism for adding to the nation's unemployment figures.

These considerations are Sally's most powerful instrument for negotiation. If she can play on management's fears of bad public relations as a result of the closure, she has some chance, however slight, of achieving a relatively harmonious outcome. A general meeting between management and employees would probably result in the union having to accept drastic cuts in wages for its members but their jobs would be saved. This would give everybody a last chance to improve productivity and keep the factory permanently in operation

— especially as such a solution would be much less costly for management in the short term, which should impress all stakeholders.

Therefore, one suggestion for the rest of the dialogue between Sally and Tony is as follows:

TONY   (as before)   Since I have already explained we are not in a position to guarantee anybody's job, I have to accept your refusal of my offer.

SALLY   (wanting to gain as widespread support as she can for the union case)   I haven't refused it. Why should I? We are in agreement that a general meeting is a good idea, so all we have to do is agree in principle how it is to be organised. Were you thinking of an open meeting, which everybody in town could attend? Personally, I think that would be great because it would give you the opportunity to explain in public exactly what your difficulties are.

TONY   (thinking of media coverage, and thinking fast)   Yes, I have in mind a public debate in the town hall. Representatives of management, and of the union, will state their positions and then the debate will be thrown open to questions from the floor and answers from the panel.

SALLY   That's a really original and innovative way to tackle the dispute. Brightrose will be a trail-blazer for industrial relations!

TONY   Yes, I think it will. Nobody will be able to say that Brightrose hasn't tried to save workers' jobs.

Further Reading

Brislin, Richard W, *The Art of Getting Things Done: A Practical Guide to the Uses of Power*, Praeger, New York, 1992

Christopher, Elizabeth M and Smith, Larry E, *Management Recruitment, Training and Development: A Sourcebook of Activities*, Kogan Page, London, 1994

—*Negotiation Training Through Gaming: Strategies, Tactics and Manœuvres*, Kogan Page, London, 1991

Downtown Planet Weekly Newspaper, Honolulu, Hawaii, week of 31 July 1995, p 4

Fisher, Roger and Ury, William, *Getting to Yes: Negotiating Agreement Without Giving in*, Penguin, London, 1988

Herzberg, Frederick, *Work and the Nature of Man*, World Publishing, New York, 1966

Herzberg, F et al, *The Motivation to Work*, Wiley, New York, 1959

Hofstede, G, 'Cultural differences in teaching and learning', *International Journal of Intercultural Relations* 10 (1986) 301–10

Jandt, Fred E, *Win–Win Negotiating: Turning Conflict into Agreement*, Wiley, New York, 1985

Le Poole, Samfrits, *Never Take No for An Answer*, (2nd edn), Kogan Page, London, 1991

Mainiero, Lisa A and Tromley, Cheryl L, *Developing Managerial Skills in Organisational Behaviour* (2nd edn), Prentice Hall, New Jersey, 1994

Milgram, Stanley, 'Behavioural Study of Obedience' in Organ, Dennis W (ed) *The Applied Psychology of Work Behaviour*, Business Studies Publications, Dallas, 1978

Sleigh, John, *Making Learning Fun*, John Sleigh Publications, Wollongong, New South Wales, Australia, 1989